DISCIPLE

The Ordinary Person's Guide to Discipling Teenagers

DISCIPLE

The Ordinary Person's Guide to Discipling Teenagers

by Dr. Allen Jackson

Foreword by Wade Morris

Disciple: The Ordinary Person's Guide To Discipling Teenagers
©2015 by Allen Jackson. All rights reserved.

Published by youthministry360 in the United States of America.

ISBN 13: 9781935832409
ISBN 10: 1935832409

PUBLISHER
Andy Blanks

GRAPHIC DESIGN
Upper Air Creative

COPY EDITOR
Kaci Hindman

SALES AND MARKETING
Les Bradford, Lee Moore, Angela Terry

*To the ordinary youth workers who
have answered an extraordinary call.*

TABLE of CONTENTS

FOREWARD

Last summer, Allen Jackson and I continued a discussion that had been ongoing between us for some time. We were at a camp together, and we were allowed to use a session to talk about the relationship between evangelism and discipleship. For the adults who were in the session, it probably looked like a tennis match. But for Allen and me, it was a rich time.

We were strengthened in our understanding that the urgent need of students taking a stand for Jesus was both immediate (evangelism) and for a lifetime (discipleship). I recognize in this book some of the concepts Allen so passionately relayed in that discussion, as well as many others. Combined, this is a great word and a great read. I love what Allen does in this book. The chapter that most reflects our discussion from that fateful camp is, "The DNA of Discipleship." I believe it is particularly helpful to a person looking for handles on the process of discipleship with students.

I would be remiss if this foreword was just about *Disciple* and not the man that wrote it. Without question, Dr. Allen Jackson has influenced, impacted, and mentored more student pastors than anyone in my generation. His position teaching youth ministry at New Orleans Baptist Theological Seminary, his experience as a student pastor, and his true depth of knowledge of the Bible, has led him to go even deeper in his teaching with this new book *Disciple*. Allen explores, among other things, the understanding of the importance of both discipleship and evangelism within the church, as well as student ministries. It is a must read for the church today.

It was quite hard to write only a few words here. I did the best I could to keep it short. I appreciate my friendship with Allen, and I appreciate this book and the place it deserves on the bookshelves of youth workers everywhere.

Wade Morris
Itinerant Minister
Wade Morris Ministries
Birmingham, Alabama
December 2014

A LETTER FROM THE AUTHOR

Dear Youth Worker,

This book is for you. I am so very aware that many, many (x100,000) books have been written on the subject of discipleship. It would be fair to ask what is different about this one. Well, for one thing it is (intentionally) shorter than most. I wanted you to be able to read it in an hour and a half. Tops. For another, it reflects many of the current discussions going on in youth ministry. It's practical. It's relevant. And it's approachable.

I believe there's also something in *Disciple* for everyone. If you're a youth ministry veteran, you'll find this book to be a good refresher on the core principles you have built your ministry on. If you're not a veteran, or if you find yourself searching for help on how to lead teenagers to become more like Christ, *Disciple* will give you a great framework for discipling teenagers. *Disciple* doesn't solve all of the theological mysteries of the universe. But it does lay down some basic principles that we can all get our minds around. The content is the result of discussions with youth ministers, parents, and students, hopefully arranged in a manner that maximizes your ability to apply it in your ministry. I pray that it's a great resource for you and for the adult volunteers on your team.

In the book, you will find theory as well as "how to." You will find a treatment of some of the classic practices of discipleship—Scripture memory, telling our stories, presenting the Gospel, etc. You will see discussions about the partnership between families and youth ministries in the discipling of students. You will see content, process, and relationship; all aimed at helping a generation mature in their faith.

I enjoyed writing *Disciple*. I hope you enjoy reading it.

Sincerely,

Dr. Allen Jackson

CHAPTER 1
INTRODUCTION

A few years ago, I wrote a book entitled, *Teach*, which had as its purpose to communicate some basic Bible study teaching ideas and techniques to people who might not have been to Bible College or Seminary. It was not meant to be highly technical or academic. In fact, my promise to readers was that they could finish the book in less than two hours. (My good friend Jim Graham edited *Teach*, and he and I talked a lot about this book. He contributed much to Chapter 5.)

The target audience for *Disciple* is similar to the target audience for *Teach*. It is either a person who enlists, equips, and encourages others to lead discipleship groups (typically a youth minister), or the actual leader of such a group (in most cases, an adult volunteer). Whatever your interest in discipleship, I hope this book is helpful. I pray that whether you are a youth minister or an adult volunteer, you would find something in this book that helps you be more effective at leading teenagers closer to Christ.

To make the reading a little easier, let's define the disciple as the one who is the learner, and the disciplemaker as the one who leads and guides the discipleship relationship. To make it even easier, I want you to intentionally picture in your mind the types of students who are open, maybe even eager, to strengthen their faith relationship with Christ. And I want to challenge you to consider that there may be more of these students in your youth group than you may think. I believe most of the teenagers in our youth ministries long to know Jesus more. I think they want a more authentic faith. And there is an interesting survey that backs this up.

In 2011, Group magazine published the findings of a survey they administered to 20,000 Christian teenagers. They gave these teenagers a list of 41 different activities they might participate in during the course of their involvement in their youth group. They asked the students to rank the ones they want more of, and the ones they want less of. The results are highly encouraging.

- 91.2% of teenagers responded that they wanted "more of" learning about Jesus. Let that sink in.

- 83.9% reported that they wanted more "Experiences that teach about God and His truths."

- 81.9% said they wanted more help learning how to pursue God on their own.

- 81.5% reported that they wanted more help in understanding the Bible.

- 74% said they wanted more opportunities for evangelism.[1]

This is an incredible response, isn't it? Many people will lament the current spiritual state of our teenagers. And while 88.9% did in fact respond that they wanted more games and fun activities (they're teenagers, after all), overall, the picture painted is of teenagers who are ready and willing to go deeper in their faith.
As you think about these responses, you might have envisioned some of the teenagers at your church. These students desire to learn significant things of God, to reflect on them, and to live them out accordingly. Don't let the image of these teenagers' faces out of your head as you read the rest of this book.

DISCIPLESHIP DEFINED

If you are reading this book, you have a heart for discipleship. But are you a disciple? For every principle we cover in this book, we'll ask two questions: How do we see this at work in the life of the disciplemaker? And how do we see it at work in the life of the disciple? But before we go on, let's get on the same page of what we mean when we talk about discipleship.

A disciple is a learner. A follower. Warren Wiersbe describes a disciple as such:
> "A disciple is a learner, one who attaches himself or herself to a teacher in order to learn a trade or subject. Perhaps our nearest modern equivalent is "apprentice," one who learns by watching and doing. The word for disciple was the most common name for the followers of Jesus Christ and is used more than 245 times in the Gospels and the Book of Acts."[2]

The word from which we get the word disciple has the same root as "discipline" and appropriately so. A while back I borrowed the title of one of Eugene Peterson's books as my definition of discipleship: A Long Obedience in the Same Direction.[3] Peterson is an author, pastor, and speaker, and this book spoke to me. It describes the journey of a pilgrim as opposed to a tourist. A pilgrim is on a quest, searching for something tangible, while a tourist walks around taking pictures and hoping he or she remembers the places they have been.

Peterson describes the journey using the Psalms of Ascent (Psalm 120-135), as these songs are the ones used by the Hebrew families as they traveled to Jerusalem for their annual pilgrimage. It is not an instant, "just add water and microwave for 30 seconds," process. These pilgrims were on the way to a holy place where they expected to meet and be met by God. They sacrificed to get there. And yet, along the way, the families who traveled together sang together: "I lift up my eyes to the hills . . . where does my help come from? My help comes from the Lord who made heaven and earth."[4] I picture the Dad asking the question, and the children answering. They were on a spiritual quest that I can pretty easily compare to discipleship.

I believe the interaction we call discipleship has a few characteristics that separate it from other types of teacher/pupil relationships:

Discipleship is intentional.
The relationship is initiated either by the disciple or the disciplemaker for the purpose of maturing toward the biblical ideal (mostly on the part of the disciple, but the disciplemaker also grows closer to Christ).

Discipleship is directional.
The disciplemaker is clearly the leader in the process, but relationship "flows" in both directions. In other words, the relationship is reciprocal. It is a two-way street, not a one-way street.

Discipleship is accountable.
Those involved in a discipleship relationship must hold each other accountable for both sin and righteousness. They must agree that they will follow through on commitments, and call each other out when they (either one) fail to do so. There should also be positive accountability in the form of praise when commitments are kept and challenges met.

Discipleship is measurable.
Both disciple and disciplemaker should ideally see progress toward specific goals.

Discipleship is seasonal.
The active, intentional meeting for the purpose of discipleship may

only last a few months or years. However the relationships last a lifetime (and possibly an eternity . . . I'll get back to you on that).

Discipleship is informational.
Truth about Scripture and life is passed from disciplemaker to disciple.

Discipleship is transformational.
A new lifestyle is learned. New habits are formed. Interactions with family, church, and culture change.

Discipleship has been compared to coaching, mentoring, teaching, and networking. I believe it lessens the importance of the discipleship relationship to compare it to terms that have secular application. I will admit that "disciple" is not an exclusively Christian concept, even though the relationship between Jesus and His closest followers is the model for this discussion. Searching for a proper metaphor, or analogy, to describe the discipleship process can be tricky.

A few years ago, several popular preachers and authors began to use a certain phrase to describe the discipleship process: "May you be covered in the dust of your rabbi." Maybe you heard this phrase when it was circulating. The idea was to describe the position of a disciple who followed so closely behind his master on a dirt road, supposedly in Palestine, that the dust kicked up by the teacher's sandals made the disciple a candidate for a bath. It is a great metaphor. The only problem is that it is pretty poor scholarship. The phrase is a mutation of a traditional rabbinic saying, and has been pretty squarely debunked as historically inaccurate.[5]

But for the sake of argument, and a good visual, let's agree that the rabbi's dust thing is a good illustration. Like other metaphors (spiritual father and son, coach and player, teacher and pupil, Obi-Wan Kenobi and Luke Skywalker), it does succeed in helping us understand the relationship between disciple and disciplemaker. The disciplemaker is the one who guides the discipleship relationship: the content, the pace, and even the direction. The disciple is the one who learns and benefits from the wisdom of the teacher, hopefully with the goal of becoming a disciplemaker in his or her own right. Paul wrote the poster-child example of this process in 2 Timothy 2:2:

> And the things you have heard me say in the presence of many witnesses entrust to reliable men who will also be qualified to teach others.

DISCIPLESHIP IS INTENTIONAL.
DISCIPLESHIP IS DIRECTIONAL.
DISCIPLESHIP IS ACCOUNTABLE.
DISCIPLESHIP IS MEASURABLE.
DISCIPLESHIP IS SEASONAL.
DISCIPLESHIP IS INFORMATIONAL.
DISCIPLESHIP IS TRANSFORMATIONAL.

I am among many Bible readers who note the four "generations" of discipleship reflected in this verse: Paul, Timothy, reliable men, and others. Paul described a process, much like a relay race (another metaphor). Each leg of the race involved a disciplemaker handing the baton to a disciple, who then became a disciplemaker, and so on.

The Bible is full of examples of such relationships. Here are just a few of the more memorable ones:

- Jethro and Moses

- Naomi and Ruth

- Elijah and Elisha

- Barnabas and Paul

- Paul and Timothy

Scripture is clear: we are called to disciple, and be discipled. The rich biblical tradition of faith transmission from person-to-person isn't some long lost ideal. It's one of the primary ways God has established for us to grow in our faith. And so, the question is: Are you a disciplemaker? One aspect of the disciplemaker's task is to say, "Come to where I am." What specific individuals have you called to your side? Another aspect of the disciplemaker's task is to say, "Come with me as I go." Who have you asked to join you on your journey?

As you ponder these questions, I'll say something that probably goes without saying (but I will say it anyway): You can't bring anybody to where you aren't. And you can't take anybody to a place to which you aren't going. In the Bible, there are lots of times when Jesus was one place, but in the next few verses, you realize He was in another place. If His disciples were going to be with Him when He changed locations, they had to move when He moved. The discipleship process is dynamic in that way.

BEGINNING WITH THE END IN MIND

Years ago, the phrase, "Beginning with the end in mind," captured my attention when I first read Steven Covey's popular book, *Seven Habits of Highly Effective People*. Covey listed this as a successful habit. The idea is that if we want to arrive at a certain destination, or achieve a certain outcome, then we identify that outcome before we start the journey. Starting a journey before you know where you're going, though fun for sight-seeing, rarely makes for a successful trip.

You may or may not know that I am a professor at the New Orleans Baptist Theological Seminary. I live on campus, in a home owned by the seminary, in a community with other faculty, staff, and students. In August 2005, I evacuated my home in New Orleans just ahead of Hurricane Katrina. The entire city, including the seminary, was flooded. I was out of my house for 13 months.

During that year, I lived with my family in a number of places, finally moving back into my home in September 2006. A large part of the stress that accompanied my "Katrina Experience" was that I felt like I was making it up as I went along. Information was hard to come by, and if someone asked me what the destination was, I couldn't say. I was on a journey that did not have a clear destination. It was not a pleasant experience.

During those "Katrina months," my goals as a child of God, husband, father, seminary professor, and friend changed almost daily as I tried to figure out how to get through the current day. With or without a hurricane, this mindset might sound familiar to many youth workers. Lacking a firm definition of ministry success, the ministry gets by based on whatever new information is provided by a publisher, website, or coffee-driven discussion with other youth ministers. Some of this information is good. Some is bad. But in this scenario, all of it is passed along absent of any plan. In this scenario, there was no starting with the end in mind.

I have a GPS unit in my car, as well as on my phone. It gives me a clue as to where I am going. But what it cannot do is to choose my destination for me. It cannot say (though it has a pleasant voice), "Allen, since you don't really know where you are going, just start driving and I will tell you when you are getting close." It can show me a map, but I have to interpret the map. It can only tell me exactly how to proceed as long as I have identified a destination.

As Hurricane Katrina meandered around in the Gulf of Mexico, the steering currents (both water and wind) were of supreme importance. These currents would direct the storm to its ultimate landfall. So to identify the steering currents was to have information needed to make a plan. Unfortunately, in youth ministry, especially as it pertains to the discipleship process, the steering currents are not so much identified as they are reacted to. For many youth workers, the buzzwords of the day (the next big thing, what the guy down the road is doing, etc.) are the currents that drive their youth ministry programming.

I don't want you to hear me making any unfair generalizations; many youth ministries are working from solid, strategic, and God-honoring planning. They have identified the currents and have recognized that they are important. These are healthy, thriving youth ministries that equip students to live dynamic faith-lives. But the struggle for a discipleship philosophy is a real issue for many youth workers. This is one reason I wrote this book. My prayer is that it will, in some way, equip youth workers like yourself with a foundation from which to build a strategic discipleship initiative at your church.

A LAST FIRST THOUGHT

I hope you are straining at the bit at the thought of initiating or refining discipleship relationships with teenagers. I don't want to throw water on the fire, but it will not be easy. Discipleship is discipline. And in Hebrews 12:11, we are reminded that "No discipline seems pleasant at the time, but painful. Later on, however, it produces a harvest of righteousness and peace for those who have been trained by it." Focusing on your own need for discipleship will not always be pleasant. Working to become a proficient disciplemaker requires great commitment. But you must remember that God has called you to this task, which means He plans on working in and through you. Take heart. You are in the perfect position to be moved and to move others.

In chapter 2, we will consider the "who" of discipleship. But first, let me ask you to slow down, breathe a little, and answer the following questions. Maybe you can even start a journal since I will ask you to stop at the end of each of these chapters and reflect a little bit. I call that section, "What about you?"

WHAT ABOUT YOU?

1. Have you ever been in a disciple/disciplemaker relationship? Write a paragraph about your memories of that relationship.

2. Why does discipleship matter? In your own words, jot down a few thoughts as to why you might want to be a part of the process.

3. If you were to ask someone to be your disciplemaker today, who would it be? Why? What would you hope to learn?

4. Are you currently discipling teenagers? If so, what is working for you? What do you see that isn't working or needs to improve?

5. Do you want to start discipling teenagers but haven't yet? Take some time to pray over your efforts, the potential students you will reach, and your own level of spiritual commitment. Commit to continuing to pray for these things.

CHAPTER 2

THE "WHO" OF DISCIPLESHIP

One of my favorite Dr. Seuss stories is *Horton Hears A Who.* If you recall, the story is about an elephant named Horton who discovers a civilization on a speck of dust. The story begins with Horton splashing around in a pool in the jungle. Suddenly, he hears a small voice calling for help. Of course, you recall, he doesn't see anyone. But he responds anyway: "I'll help you," said Horton. "But who are you? Where?"[1] Horton quickly realizes that the voice is coming from a speck of dust floating through the air.

A few paragraphs later, the elephant Horton realized that someone or something was on that speck of dust and it needed his help. He utters the fairly famous line, "A person is a person no matter how small," then engages the voice in dialogue. Horton comes to realize that there is indeed a microscopic civilization on this speck of dust, a civilization that could use his help. This initial exchange ends with Horton making a promise, of sorts, to the Mayor of the town: "You're safe now. Don't worry. I won't let you down."

You're safe. I won't let you down. When we are confident in the person saying those words, they provide immense comfort. Students may never acknowledge the comfort and assurance they feel when an adult disciplemaker conveys those sentiments, but I am convinced they need to hear them. The pace of our students' world is breathtakingly faster than it was just a few decades ago. The myriad of choices, the relentless flow of information, and the instant gratification of the culture combine to make us wonder if a disciplemaker can compete. I believe we can. But we have to start with an understanding of who students are, who we are, and how the discipleship relationship can give some guidance to the "whos" gathered on this speck of dust we call church.

THE WHOS ARE CHANGING

There is a lot of talk about the rapid changes we've seen in this generation of teenagers. And for good reason. Culture is advancing at a rapid rate. But if all we do is focus on the changes that are happening outside teenagers, we miss many of the internal changes. And these changes are some of the most significant when it comes to teenagers growing and maturing. It is said that more changes take place during adolescence than any other time in life, except for infancy. (I wrote an e-book awhile back that gives a much more detailed description of these changes. I have provided a link to a free download in chapter 6.)

The five basic areas of human development are physical, mental, social, emotional, and spiritual. When we apply these areas of growth to teenagers, most of us will agree that physical growth is the most evident, and emotional growth is the most frustrating (for students, parents, and/or youth workers). I want to briefly focus on the last area, that of spiritual formation. But not before taking a refresher course on adolescent development.

There is a quote I love that I believe has been attributed to Og Mandino, though, I have been unable to definitively track down its source. It goes something like this: "We aren't human beings. We are humans becoming." Wow! What a thought. And one that sums up the process we find our students undergoing during their adolescent years. Our students are constantly changing, and if you're lucky enough to have a long tenure at a church, you can watch this change happen right before your eyes. Let's take a moment and run through the different stages of development.

Consider preteens. They are just entering the drama called adolescence. Their bodies will change a lot in just a few months (the growth spurt). Physically and socially, the girls are almost always ahead of the guys in development. Spiritually, preteens are beginning to realize that choices are becoming complicated, and that they can, and do, choose to sin. For teenagers who have made professions of faith, assurance of salvation is a concept that needs to be reinforced. For teenagers who have not made a decision to trust Christ, a clear presentation of the Gospel with understandable, concrete theological explanation is vital.

Continue on to middle school. Guys are catching up developmentally with the girls. Socially, most middle schoolers still prefer same-sex friends. Emotionally, hormones are raging. Spiritual conversations may have to fight through the clutter of the awakening to the hormone-induced awareness of the opposite sex. Spiritual questions may revolve around hypothetical situations, and some false information may be introduced via Internet "research." According to almost every study, parents are the primary spiritual guides for adolescents at this age. Adults are respected, and often sought. Intentional and challenging discipleship at church creates platforms for interaction.

The high school years may be the most critical for discipleship. Physical change is leveling out, emotional upheaval is somewhat stabilized, and confidence is growing in mental abilities. Spiritually, some key developments occur. I polled the classes I teach at the seminary, and about 75% of my students (studying to be ministers) indicated that something happened in the 9th or 10th grade that changed or challenged their spiritual maturity. They indicated that they understood a call to ministry, repented of lifestyle choices that did not glorify God, or decided to "get serious" about their faith. I believe that much of this data indicates an increasing ability to think abstractly. In our youth ministries, we should be honest about the messiness of our world, and challenge them to believe that God is in control.

Now that we have covered some of the bigger picture developmental markers, let us focus on the spiritual development of our students. It is easy to see development in the other areas we discussed earlier, but how do we observe spiritual formation? We can celebrate the first steps of a baby, or the first shave of an adolescent (physical development), but can we measure spiritual "firsts"?

I would answer, "definitely." But measuring spiritual growth is unlike measuring physical growth, or cognitive (mental) growth. My children both have graduated marks on the frames of their bedroom doors, signifying their change in height from one year (month, week, good grief!) to the next. What would the spiritual comparison be? A mark for entering into a saving relationship with Christ? Sure. In my denomination, and maybe yours, we might add another mark for baptism. Wouldn't we add a mark for a teenager standing up in front of your church and giving a testimony following a mission trip? I think so. Leading a friend to Christ, showing great empathy for the lost and/or outcast, initiating a Bible study group, taking greater ownership of their personal time in Scripture reading and prayer, and so on. All of these are signs of spiritual growth.

Here's a truth: Anything that is not growing is not natural. We must expect growth in our students. And a lack of growth in specific students is something we should address. But there are some thoughts to consider as we begin to observe the spiritual growth of our students.

Unlike physical and possibly mental development, the sequence of spiritual change is not predictable. Rapid spiritual growth does not necessarily follow conversion, and depends significantly on actions of parents, pastors, and friends. That is what makes describing spiritual development kind of a like trying to hold a raw oyster. (Sorry, my Louisiana roots are showing.) A look at some of the adults in our churches may lead one to believe that growth toward spiritual maturity can be slow, and perhaps even optional. In addition, people come to Christ as Savior at different points in their lives. Therefore, a person celebrating their first "spiritual birthday" may be eight-years-old or forty-eight-years old.

Here's another reason it is tricky to think about spiritual growth as a linear process: While spirituality is not a minor story with today's adolescents, it doesn't anchor many of their lives either. The *National Study on Youth and Religion* (www.youthandreligion.org) found that most teenagers believed in God at some level, but only 1 in 10 would be described as "devoted" to their faith. They do not equate their spiritual growth with church attendance, and they largely believe that their faith runs in the background, rather than influencing day-to-day decisions. For most of them, their moral decision-making is not necessarily guided by their relationship with God. Part of our challenge as youth workers is to "connect the dots," helping them unify life and faith.

So that is a look at some of the developmental changes teenagers are experiencing. Let's continue our look at the "whos" of discipleship by looking at some of the characteristics of this generation of teenagers.

THE WHOS ARE COMPARTMENTALIZING

Back in high school, I took, and miraculously passed, geometry class. I was fascinated by something called a "Venn Diagram," which basically taught about sets of things that have overlap. Set A overlapped with Set B, which overlapped with Set C. The interesting area was that part that contained some of all the sets. It looked like this:

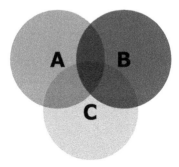

Follow me here. If "A" is a teenager's school, or work world, and "B" is a teenager's family, and/or community world, and "C" is church world, it would seem logical that this teenager would have an overlap, so that his or her identity as a Christ-follower would extend into the other "worlds." Instead, many teenagers have perfected the art of keeping their "worlds" separate.

If we are to truly understand discipleship, we have to come to grips (as adult disciples) that our discipleship extends into all of our worlds. I would not promote us being obnoxious or rude, but we have to "de-compartmentalize" if we wish to create significant discipleship environments for students.

Think of it this way: I am a minister, a professor, a writer, a speaker, a runner, a (very bad) golfer, and probably some other roles I cannot think of. You might be an accountant, an executive, a business owner, a lawyer, a teacher, a butcher, baker, or a candlestick maker. But the discipleship question asks: What is your primary role? Are you a lawyer, or teacher who happens to go to a church, or a Bible study? Or are you a follower of Christ who happens to be a lawyer or teacher? The difference is subtle but significant. If you are a Christ-follower who happens to be in another occupation, then you take your discipleship to work with you.

If you take your discipleship to work with you, then you aren't the "Jeckyl and Hyde," or "Transformer" kind of Christian who keeps faith in the church and out of other areas of life. If you take your discipleship to work with you, to your home with you, to the golf course, or mall with you, then you are the kind of disciple who provides a model of consistency to the younger "whos" who desperately need it.

THE WHOS ARE CONFLICTED

The students in our churches (and in the culture outside the church) aren't predictable, and they differ from one part of the country (or world) to another. And we should always make a disclaimer when we begin to paint a generation of teenagers using a broad brush. We should recognize that the collective group of teenagers in our country is made up of individuals who defy generalization. And yet, we can make some big picture cultural statements about teenagers as a demographic. For instance, this generation of teenagers tends to be independent and insecure all at the same time. They are not afraid to attempt challenges alone

BUILDING RELATIONSHIPS IS THE KEY TO UNDERSTANDING THE STUDENTS YOU DISCIPLE.

RELATIONSHIPS BETWEEN ADULTS AND STUDENTS ARE FOUNDATIONAL TO THE PROCESS.

(or with friends), but they use their cell phone to call their parents almost daily. They are generally confident and tolerant, but also narcissistic and in need of social validation.

When you observe this generation of students, you cannot help but be amazed. They are industrious, creative, and talented. Yet they are connected to some screen almost constantly. And one of the main characterizations of this generation is that they are conflicted.

In an article for NBC.com, writer Tracy Connor described millennials, those individuals born between 1980 and 2000. Her description of millennials is fascinating and represents the overall tone of much of the research done on this demographic. While some of what Connor writes applies to young adults, she captures some of the conflicted nature that so many of our teenagers have when it comes to issues such as morality, politics, and faith:

> [Statistically, millennials] are more often than not white and unmarried, but hoping to tie the knot down the road. They describe themselves as politically independent, but lean Democratic . . . They prefer bigger government to fewer services, and think the powers-that-be should be spending more money on them, but they're not so sure about Obamacare . . . Their social views are progressive and have become more liberal over time. Support gay marriage? Yep. Support legal pot? You bet. In favor of legal status for undocumented immigrants? Check. They believe in God, at least they think they do. But don't call them religious. Don't call them an environmentalist, either, and flip a coin before labeling them a patriot. They have never known life without the Internet . . . but also have some misgivings about technology.[2]

Like I said, you can't make too much of anyone's generalization of a generation (mine included). But what we can say about this generation of teenagers is that they are a product of arguably the most rapidly changing culture in our country's history. Against this backdrop, how can we hope to connect with them in ways that foster discipleship? I contend that building relationships is the key to understanding the students you are able to disciple. Relationships between adults and students are foundational to the process.

It's important to remember that we adults have not "graduated" from change, conflict, or compartmentalization. Our bodies are changing too. We are conflicted about different things. And much of the compartmentalization displayed by the students was learned from us! But when we realize that we are adults who are on the journey of discipleship, leading students on a journey of discipleship, the terrifying part of it melts away. The students just need to catch us being disciples.

ON GENERATIONAL DISCIPLESHIP

Avery Willis Jr. said, "Discipleship is developing a personal, life-long, obedient relationship with Jesus Christ in which He transforms your character into Christlikeness; changes your values to Kingdom values; and involves you in His mission in the home, in the church, and in the world."[3] In the passage we looked at earlier, in his words to Timothy, the Apostle Paul suggested that discipleship was meant to be passed on from one believer to another. Paul was clearly concerned about the relationships that pass faith from one generation to the next.

As a youth ministry professor, I plan my classes around trying to describe ways to help students and their families in the context of the church, and the culture, to see that faith is passed from one generation to the next. Probably the most famous verse that points us in that direction is what our Jewish brothers and sisters call the Shema, from the Hebrew word for "hear," from Deuteronomy. The Hebrews needed instruction as to how they would live when they finally got to the Promised Land. And so God reminded them that families are the best way to pass along meaning, faith, culture, and love.

> Hear, O Israel: The LORD our God, the LORD is one. Love the LORD your God with all your heart and with all your soul and with all your strength. These commandments that I give you today are to be upon your hearts. Impress them on your children. Talk about them when you sit at home and when you walk along the road, when you lie down and when you get up. Tie them as symbols on your hands and bind them on your foreheads. Write them on the doorframes of your houses and on your gates. - Deuteronomy 6:4-9

I love this. I can hear the clear call for a spiritually strong father to joyfully and determinedly declare to his family that they will love God with all their hearts. I get excited at the declarations recorded in Exodus and Deuteronomy and Joshua that have children excitedly asking their fathers about the great things that God has done. Notice the emphasis (mine):

- In days to come, **when your son asks** you, "What does this mean?" say to him, "With a mighty hand the LORD brought us out of Egypt, out of the land of slavery. - Exodus 13:14

- In the future, **when your son asks** you, "What is the meaning of the stipulations, decrees and laws the LORD our God has commanded you?" tell him . . . - Deuteronomy 6:20-21

- In the future, **when your children ask** you, 'What do these stones mean?' tell them . . . - Joshua 4:6-7

Can't you just see the family devotion time wrapped around the amazing miracles at the Red Sea and the Jordan River? The Shema teaches that these stories of God's greatness are to be built into the catechism of the home. But also built in is the assumption that parents and adults in the faith community were continuing to mature spiritually throughout life. God's ideal assumes that children will ask the meaning of spiritual events because they believe their parents can answer their questions. That assumption may no longer be true.

I have heard many youth ministers express their spiritual goals for their students in terms of things like: "When students graduate from high school, I want them to be able to recognize and respond to the lordship of Christ, practice spiritual disciplines, develop and demonstrate Christ's character, make wise decisions, develop godly relationships, make an intentional impact on others, and so on." Great thoughts. But as we begin to transition away from the who of discipleship and into the what, we need to make sure that the partnership between youth ministry and family tilts towards family.

While most recent and credible research points to the role of parents as most effective disciplemakers of students, research also raises a question. With the spiritual giants of the Silent Generation now living as grandparents, the question is whether the Baby Boomers and the Generation X-ers will be mature enough in their faith to take the lead in discipling their preschoolers, adolescents, and teenagers. It is a challenge for pastors, youth pastors, and adult volunteers alike.

Such discipleship of adults must be initiated by the Pastor. He is the chief disciplemaker of the church. And disciples do not live by sermons alone. Dr. Avery Willis, Jr. was asked if pastors can disciple their congregation solely from the pulpit through the weekly preaching event. The way I heard the story (actually told in his book, *Truth That Sticks*) is that Dr. Willis responded with something like, "Preaching is like spraying milk out upon babies hoping that they will catch something in their mouth. Discipling involves one-on-one, or face-to-face relationship and communication." It is ridiculous to spray milk on babies and call it nutrition. It is equally ridiculous to think of relying solely on one-way communication for discipleship.

So we have work to do. To claim that youth ministry is a failed experiment because students statistically are not describing faith in the terms the researchers are looking for is not the whole story. Granted, young adults do not embrace the traditional church in the same way that previous generations have done. But they are a deeply spiritual generation. What we know for sure is that churches–pastors, youth pastors, worship leaders, deacons, and all other leaders–are stakeholders in the future of their faith communities to the degree that they take seriously the Great Commission imperative to make disciples.

The rest of this book is devoted to that aim. We've laid the foundation. Now let's begin to transition to the practical application of disciplemaking.

WHAT ABOUT YOU?

1. Why is it sometimes frustrating to watch teenagers struggle to develop spiritually? Articulate your response in two or three main words.

2. Have you seen evidence of compartmentalization in your students? How might you and your team address this in your students?

3. Do you see compartmentalization in your own life? What are some areas in which your identity as a Christ-follower needs to overlap more?

4. On a scale of 1 to 10, with 1 being "very good" and 10 being "needs some work," describe how well your youth ministry "tilts" toward supporting discipleship in the home.

CHAPTER 3

THE DNA OF DISCIPLESHIP

I have been fascinated with genetics since I was in grade school. (True confession: I took as much biology as I could in high school so I could avoid chemistry.) In my lifetime, science has made incredible progress in understanding how fearfully and wonderfully God made us. I am encouraged by the combined efforts of medicine and science as the genetic code is decoded, and horrible genetic diseases are treated.

One of the more significant discoveries is how our genetic blueprint is tied to our deoxyribonucleic acid, or DNA. As we know, DNA is a molecule containing the genetic instruction code for humans. The familiar double helix design of DNA is widely understood to be responsible for what makes us who we are, at least from a genetic standpoint.

In many conversations today, we hear something like this: "Well that's just part of our DNA," or "The way we do things is in our DNA." We use phrases like these to describe the core infrastructure of an organization, a program, or even a church ("our worship style is just our DNA"). Since the term is already in use to describe values at the core of a thought or organization, I feel relatively comfortable trying to identify the strands of DNA for the process we call discipleship.

By way of introduction, I believe the five "strands," or core aspects, of discipleship are as follows:

- Knowing God's Word (Scripture memory)

- Knowing God's Story (Understanding the story, or meta-narrative, of the Bible)

- Telling Our Story (Articulating a "testimony")

- Sharing The Gospel With Words (Evangelism)

- Sharing The Gospel With Deeds (Gospel-centered social justice/compassion)

The remainder of this chapter will explore each strand. My hope is that by breaking down the task of discipleship into the desired outcomes, we can reduce the intimidation factor and get to work. You will notice that for each of these strands, I talk about what a specific strand means for you, the disciplemaker, and for your students, the disciples. Some youth workers are guilty of looking for a plan to lead their students closer to Christ while ignoring their own spiritual journey. As I said earlier in the book, you can't lead someone to a place you haven't been. While we can never discount the work of the Holy Spirit in making us like Christ, if we're not disciples ourselves, our disciplemaking efforts will be severely inhibited.

Now, let's dig in.

STRAND 1: KNOWING GOD'S WORD
(SCRIPTURE MEMORY)

The Why of Scripture Memory
One of the casualties of our "Google culture," where we do not have to memorize anything except our password to get into our list of passwords, is that we downplay the value of memorizing anything. If we can access it, why clutter up our minds with it? My hope is that you might become a fan of memorizing Scripture almost as a way of being countercultural! And I sincerely hope you lead your students to do the same.

I think when our students memorize Scripture, it helps them to separate the content of the Bible from so many other books, magazines, web pages, other entertainment sources, and just random information. In a world where their Bible app sits next to Snapchat and the Kim Kardashian Hollywood game on their phones, Scripture memory creates a sense of the sacred in a way that reading a Bible on a screen doesn't.

Both you and your students are bombarded by words and images all day, everyday. If we want to lead teenagers to a deep discipleship, it is vital for you and them to read, hear, and memorize the Word. We quote Psalm 119:11 a lot to help make the biblical case for this practice. Consider the way different translations deal with the verse:

- **New International Version**
  I have hidden your word in my heart that I might not sin against you.

- **English Standard Version**
  I have stored up your word in my heart, that I might not sin against you.

- **New American Standard Revised Edition**
  Your word I have treasured in my heart, that I may not sin against You.

- **King James Version**
  Thy word have I hid in mine heart, that I might not sin against thee.

The writer of the psalm wrote that he had hidden, stored, and treasured the Scripture, with the end result that his behavior was impacted. The 19th Century Scottish minister, author, and hymnist, Horatius Bonar, built on the sentiment the psalmist expressed when he wrote, "We must study the Bible more. We must not only lay it up within us, but transfuse it through the whole texture of the soul."[1] Even Jesus quoted Scripture in a time of temptation. In the wilderness, He answered Satan's twisted offer with Scripture. Though Jesus is Himself the Word of God, He used the written Word of God for battling temptation.

As we consider the practice of memorizing Scripture ourselves, or talk to our students about it, we should not jump to thinking that it works like some magic chant. We should, however, jump to stories of captured soldiers in places where they were not allowed to have a Bible, but who were able to hang on to hope because they had committed it to memory. We should jump to our own experiences where a verse or a Scripture-based song gave us comfort and hope because it came to mind in a dark or desperate time. Chuck Swindoll wrote,

> "I know of no other single practice in the Christian life more rewarding, practically speaking, than memorizing Scripture . . . No other single exercise pays greater spiritual dividends! Your prayer life will be strengthened. Your witnessing will be sharper and much more effective. Your attitudes and outlook will begin to change. Your mind will become alert and observant. Your confidence and assurance will be enhanced. Your faith will be solidified."[2]

We should jump to the promise that memorizing Scripture keeps us closer to purity and obedience (for us and our students). "How can a young man keep his way pure? By guarding it according to your word" (Psalm 119:9). Knowing God's Word through memorization of Bible verses is a mental check that helps us and our students guard our lives and actions. When God's Word is fresh in our minds, we are more likely to choose God's way in our daily routine.

There are a few places in the Bible itself where we either observe someone quoting Scripture, or we are told to commit it to memory. First and foremost, Jesus memorized Scripture. He quoted the Old Testament frequently (obviously, the New Testament wasn't written yet). In His life and ministry, He quoted from 24 different books roughly 180 times! It is clear that He respected the thought of the Scriptures as the ultimate authority in life, and a way to understand the heart and desires of the Father. Why would we not follow Jesus by knowing and trusting Scripture the way He did?

If we believe the Bible to be inspired by God, we should take it seriously. And we should lead our students to do the same:

- For the word of God is living and active. Sharper than any double-edged sword, it penetrates even to dividing soul and spirit, joints and marrow; it judges the thoughts and attitudes of the heart. - Hebrews 4:12

- But as for you, continue in what you have learned and have become convinced of, because you know those from whom you learned it, and how from infancy you have known the holy Scriptures, which are able to make you wise for salvation through faith in Christ Jesus. All Scripture is God-breathed and is useful for teaching, rebuking, correcting and training in righteousness, so that the man of God may be thoroughly equipped for every good work. - 2 Timothy 2:14-17

- Above all, you must understand that no prophecy of Scripture came about by the prophet's own interpretation. For prophecy never had its origin in the will of man, but men spoke from God as they were carried along by the Holy Spirit. - 2 Peter 1:20-21

Simply put, we are called to memorize Scripture.

Want more evidence? Colossians 3:16 tells us to "let the word of Christ dwell in us richly." Deuteronomy 6:4-9 tells us that God's Word is to be written on our hearts, and that we are to impress it on our children, talking about it in our homes and as we go from place to place. We must know Scripture first before we can teach it or apply it as God desires. Romans 12:1-2 tells is to be transformed by the renewing of our minds, testing and discerning God's will. Memorizing Scripture renews our mind and transforms your life and the lives of your students.

In Ephesians 6:10-20, we enjoy the description of the protection God gives us through righteousness, salvation, truth, and willingness to share the Gospel. Only one offensive weapon is mentioned: "the sword of the Spirit, which is the Word of God." We all want our teenagers to make an impact on their worlds for the sake of Christ. When they memorize Bible passages, we have a powerful offensive weapon to answer false or tempting words. If they know Scripture, in both tough and opportune times alike, their words will be God's Words! Knowing Bible verses about temptation, spiritual struggle, and our protection from God is like swinging a powerful blade in a tough culture. The Word has power!

One more "why" and I will move on to the "how" regarding Scripture memory. Memorizing Scripture helps us to encourage believers and witness to non-believers. When we have put the Word in our hearts, it can come back out in a way that can encourage fellow disciples to live in obedience, fight temptation, work through a difficult time, and conform more to the person of Christ. I don't know about you, but I am in favor of leading students to equip themselves to reach each other and to reach the lost. Helping them grasp the importance of Scripture memory is vital.

When disciples help other disciples with accountability, Scripture helps in keeping our opinions out of the way and letting God's opinion move to the front. Paul told the church to be ready to encourage other believers with the truth (1 Thess 4:18). We've already noted where he told Timothy that "all Scripture is useful for teaching, reproof, correction, and training in righteousness" (2 Tim 3:16). Knowing Scripture is key in ministering to others.

Finally, memorizing Scripture allows you and your students to share with non-believers. In order "to always be ready to give a defense for our hope in Christ" (1 Pet 3:15), you should memorize Scripture so you can answer questions respectfully and confidently, while pointing non-believers to the grace that Jesus offers. You should equip and challenge your students to do the same. If you have committed relevant texts to memory, you are less "canned" and more able to lead someone to faith conversationally. This is especially true for your students.

If we're honest, we will admit that many of our students profess difficulty in memorizing Scripture. They (and maybe us too) claim that they just don't have the capacity. At the risk of using an illustration that will quickly become dated, please allow an observation. I am a fan of baseball at any level. Not long ago, I was in Mobile, AL to watch a minor league game. It happened to be a day game, and also "kid's day," which means that the upper deck was pretty much full of children from day camps, sports camps, church groups, and other collections of young humans.

During a break between innings, a song from the movie, *Frozen* came on the loudspeakers, inspiring an impromptu sing-a-long. Every child knew every word of every verse. I am not exaggerating. The (20-something) ushers led the way as the children sang and danced, belting out,

> "Let it go. Let it go! /
> And I'll rise like the break of dawn. /
> Let it go. Let it go! /
> That perfect girl is gone!"

As I write this, I have yet to see the movie. I am not sure if the perfect girl went somewhere, or ceased to be perfect. But that's not really my point. As I think back on the thousand or so children singing in unison, I am quite sure that you and your teenagers have the capacity to memorize Scripture. Most of us don't have a convincing argument for why we do not have the capacity to memorize God's Word when we set our minds, voices, and emotions to it. This is a good segue to the second section part of this section: the "how" of memorizing Scripture.

The How of Scripture Memory
How can we help our teenagers begin to memorize God's Word? I won't be able to list all of the many ways here. To keep from overwhelming you, dear reader, with lists, below I have given you my top five. But if you search for "Scripture Memory Strategies," you will find pages of advice as to how people have committed Bible verses to memory. I highly encourage you to do such a search, but only once or twice. The goal is to find out what works for you and your students and get started. Don't waste time and energy trying to find the "perfect" plan. The best thing you can do for your students is to get started.

1. Read it.

Andy Blanks, co-founder of youthministry360 (the organization that published this book), and one of my former students, has a saying when he speaks to youth ministers about strategies to help their students engage with the Bible: "The trick to creating a hunger in your students for reading God's Word is for them to simply read God's Word." Andy is alluding to the fact that Scripture isn't like any other kind of literature. It is "living and active" (Heb. 4:12). Plus, we have the Spirit working behind the scenes to illuminate the truth so that we are transformed by it. The act of memorizing Scripture occurs in a similar context.

The first step in memorizing Scripture is to read Scripture. (Funny concept, I know.) Sometimes when we read Scripture, we want to get finished as if we are checking off a task. This is especially true about many of our teenagers. But slowing down and getting a feel for a passage is crucial. Encourage the following techniques in your students. When they are drawn to a verse or a passage, encourage them to read it several times. Read it aloud. Challenge them to copy the verses into a journal (or in my case a planner). Maybe, like me, they could use a highlighter to color verses or passages that get their attention while reading devotionally. I have heard of people writing the verse on their bathroom mirror with a dry-erase marker in order to read it even more. (Choose your marker wisely.) When they discover a verse that seems very relevant to something in their lives, they have found a good place to start.

2. Strategize it.

As with anything, a new discipline needs a plan. Many people use memory cards, phone apps, or post-it notes strategically to place verses they want to memorize in front of them on a constant basis. Biblegateway.com had a great hint for a beginner:

> "Start small. Choose a short verse to start with . . . and make it even shorter by breaking it down into pieces. Memorize the first five words in the verse first, and when you've got them down, add the next five. As you become more confident, you can add more words, sentences, and even entire verses—but don't add anything new until you've got the previous words down pat."[3]

Start small, but work your way large. This is great advice as you're trying to build this habit in your students. It is rewarding and inspiring to memorize a larger portion of Scripture, like an entire psalm, or a chapter from one of Paul's letters. Memorizing larger chunks also gives a greater sense of context that we might miss by quoting a verse. But we want students to be successful and to feel like this is something achievable. Having success with some smaller passages is the way to go.

3. Pray it.
I spoke at a youth camp this past summer and a student asked me how to battle pride. I told her that she was asking the right person! In some of the many times that I have been convicted of being prideful, I opened the Bible to Psalm 51 and prayed to have God's perspective. I pray that He would "renew a right spirit in me." I have prayed that psalm so many times that I have much of it memorized!

One way to lead your students to see some fruit when it comes to memorizing Scripture is to encourage them to seek out verses or passages that address an area of struggle in their lives. Not only will this encourage them to be a little more spiritually invested in the process, it will consistently put them in the place to interact with the conviction of the Spirit through God's Word.

4. Quote it.
Drive time is an excellent time to say your verses out loud to yourself. Help encourage students to find similar moments in their days where they can say their verses out loud. Saying verses out loud to others is also effective. One of the most impressive youth group sermons I ever saw was when a group of students in New Orleans quoted the entire Book of Philippians to their church during a worship service. They quoted it relay-style with one student saying 5-10 verses followed by another and another until they quoted the whole book. Maybe biting off the entire Book of Philippians is ambitious for your group. Maybe not. The point is that there is something about speaking the verses that aids in memorization. Speaking the words out loud gives us motivation and accountability (and maybe even a little bit of healthy anxiety, if it's in front of a group.)

5. Sing it.
Let's face it. We know lots of verses because we know them as songs. Scripture-based songs appeal to a different part of our brain and it never hurts to use more brain cells. Help your students find praise songs that contain Scripture. Want to know a real tip? When nobody is looking, load your i-thing with Scripture songs from a children's collection. (The fine folks at seedsfami-

lyworship.com are amazing at this. You can find their music on Pandora, Spotify, iTunes, etc. But I'm warning you: you WILL be singing them all day.) If your students are feeling bold, challenge them to make up their own songs, putting Bible verses to a tune they already know.

As a bonus, I might add, teach it. If you or your students prepare to teach, you always learn better. Encourage students to plan to quote a passage in the study you are leading. Or better yet, equip a student to teach for you. I go back to our friends from biblegateway.com for the conclusion:

> If you've never tried memorizing a Bible verse before, it's much easier than you think . . . One thing is certain: you'll never regret spending more time focusing intently on God's Word. And there's nothing quite so wonderful as an encouraging Bible verse springing forth from memory at just the time you need to hear it.

STRAND 2: KNOWING THE META-NARRATIVE OF THE BIBLE

When I first considered this strand in the DNA of discipleship, I was thinking of a natural extension of Scripture memory. I was thinking about the ability of a Christ-follower to understand the Bible as a whole story, and not a series of disconnected parts. We need to understand that the Bible is a document that God inspired to be written by humans, for humans, and with the understanding that humans would change over the centuries. For many readers, the Bible is just a collection of random stories or even more random verses. Stepping back from the individual verses and stories, though, a unity is apparent.

The word "meta-narrative" has been used to describe the "big story," or "grand narrative," of the Bible. The meta-narrative is the thread that explains and connects many little stories. The meta-narrative of the Bible is its story of Jesus, God's self-revelation to the world.

A disciple should have an awareness of the whole Bible, not in a frightening way, but in a way that sees God's love and purpose whether you are reading the words of Moses, Malachi, or Matthew. One of my preaching professor friends told me that what I was really talking about was hermeneutics, or, "The process of interpretation to understand an author's intended original meaning."

What I understand him to say is that we need to know the assumptions, or rules, we use to study and interpret the Bible. We assume that God inspired the Bible. We assume that God had in mind that Jesus would be sent to die for our sins. We assume that the relationship between God and man is personal. We assume that the starting point to understanding Scripture is to consider other Bible passages.

There are other assumptions:
- The author had a clear and objective meaning and purpose in mind when recording his thoughts.

- The author used language and structures that were meaningful and understandable to the original intended audience.

- That objective meaning and purpose can be known, and is anchored in history (this avoids a reader-response, or a subjective approach to studying the Bible).

- We assume that God is consistent in character, and that His character, as revealed through His actions in history (recorded in Scripture), remains consistent with contemporary circumstances.

That's a lot to take in, isn't it? Hermeneutics is a word that describes the way theology interacts with the principles of interpreting the Bible. In a word, it is an approach to looking at all of Scripture. It is a tool used to understand the meta-narrative of the Bible.

As I begin to shift toward dealing with how you might begin helping your students learn and appreciate the big-picture story of Scripture, there are at least three challenges commonly identified as hurdles to a clear understanding the Bible. First, the Old Testament was written in Hebrew, and the New Testament was written in Greek and Aramaic. Unless your students are really, really extraordinary, these are all foreign languages to them. Second, you and your students have to struggle with how much a dynamic world impacts our study; what are the timeless principles and what principles have to be considered in light of ever-changing culture? Finally, we remember that the events of the Bible happened thousands of years ago, and over the period of several thousand years.

My point here is that many teenagers are simply intimidated by the Bible. And yet, they don't have to be. God meant for us ordinary people to understand it. The main way we can help students to see the big picture of Scripture, without the intimidation factor, is to approach the Bible as a whole story. Even though the types of literature represented in the Bible range from history, to biography, to poetry, to prophecy, to gospel, and to epistle, the Old and New Testaments come together to tell the story of God at work among men.

Now let me back away from theory and suggest a framework for you to use to see what God is saying through all the individual stories and events recorded. One way to teach a particular passage in light of the meta-narrative of the Scripture is to use both deductive and inductive technique. Deductive study is like Sherlock Holmes. You find a clue in a verse or passage, and look for the bigger meaning. Inductive study is like Google earth. You start with a wide shot–a chapter, verse, or type of Scripture–and try to land on the guiding principle or theme.

Inductive Bible Study (inductive means "general to specific") is often described as a process of observation, interpretation, and application. In this process, you help students observe the structure, the big picture, determine word meanings, time frames, geographical locations, people relationships, the author and audience, the type of Scripture, and the text itself. An attempt is made to interpret how all of these observations point to a meaning or interpretation. Finally, a conclusion is suggested as to what persons should think, do, or feel as a result of understanding the text more clearly.

Deductive Bible Study (deductive means specific to general) usually begins from a pre-assigned point (a verse or a topic to investigate), and then examines the Scripture in a widening arc to determine the instruction or conclusion from the Bible regarding the inquiry. Deductive Bible study provides general principles regarding a specific point. It is probably the most well-known and used technique in pastoral ministry. For example, I might read the shortest verse in the Bible, John 11:35, and ask, "Why did Jesus weep?" As I widened my search, I would discover His love for a friend who had died, as well as a passion for people who did not understand the Gospel.

I realize that many of you may very well be handed a Bible study lesson by your youth minster that he or she has written himself or herself, or you may teach from a published curriculum that is similarly provided you. What if there is no consideration given in these lessons to the big-picture story of Scripture? First, you can (and should) always adapt what you are given to incorporate some of these practices just mentioned. But there are also a few simple techniques you can implement to draw your students' attention out of a specific passage and help them see where the passage falls in the meta-narrative of Scripture.

Before you teach any Bible verse or passage, take a moment to place the book of the Bible that verse or passage is in into the overall timeline of Scripture. It can look as simple as something like this:

> "Today we'll be looking at a few verses from Romans. If we're thinking about where Romans falls in the Bible, it's a New Testament book. The Apostle Paul wrote Romans roughly thirty years after Jesus died. The Church had started to spread after Jesus' death and resurrection. Romans was written to these new Christ-followers who were living in Rome."

If you do something similar to this, you've helped place the book in context with the rest of Scripture. Your students would know that Romans isn't in the Old Testament. Paul wasn't a contemporary of Job. He was writing after Jesus had lived, died, and resurrected. This kind of simple contextual information is critical to helping your students understand how the narrative of Scripture works. Do this enough with the different lessons you teach, and you will very organically help your students grasp the flow of the Bible's story.

Here's another "help." Go a step further and help your students grasp the particulars of a book as you teach it. Do this by answering three simple questions:

- Who wrote the book?

- When was it written?

- Why was it written? (In other words, what's its purpose?)

Students need to know that God-inspired people wrote Scripture with a specific purpose in mind, in a certain cultural context. Filling in these simple facts as you teach helps teenagers grasp the unique and specific nature of the various books of the Bible.

Finally, one of the most important things to remember when helping students attempt to grasp the meta-narrative of Scripture is to look for how the Gospel speaks into, or influences, or reframes the specific passage of Scripture you are studying. One of the foundational truths of the Bible is that Jesus can be found from Genesis to Revelation. The thread of God's redemptive love for His children courses through the Bible. We see shades of the Gospel in the Creation account, in the Fall, in the stories of Abraham, Isaac, Jacob, Joseph, David, the Prophets, and so on. As you teach Scripture, look for how the Gospel intersects with the passage you are studying, and bring this to students' attention. (As an aside, one of the most helpful resources for seeing the Gospel thread in Scripture is the wonderful *ESV Gospel Transformation Bible* from Crossway. It's worth a look.)

In 1 Corinthians 2:12-13 Paul penned, "We have not received the spirit of the world but the Spirit who is from God, that we may understand what God has freely given us. This is what we speak, not in words taught us by human wisdom but in words taught by the Spirit, expressing spiritual truths in spiritual words."

The Bible is meant to be understood and God's story is meant to be retold. If we want to see our students become disciples, this is a truth they must embrace.

STRAND 3: TELLING OUR STORY
(ARTICULATING A "TESTIMONY")

One of the most powerful ways to lead a person in a discipleship relationship is for you to tell, and for them to hear, your story. And one of the most powerful ways our teenagers can lead others to Christ is for their peers to hear their story. Story cuts through the "noise" of our world like nothing else. Advertisers and marketers know something about this generation of young people: they are drawn to story. And those of us who are Christ-followers, simply by way of coming to a saving faith in Jesus, have amazing stories.

Such a story is recorded in John 9, the personal and emotional testimony from a man that Jesus healed from blindness. Apparently, the man was in the right place at the right time, and as Jesus and His disciples were walking down the road, they came across this fellow.

1 As he went along, he saw a man blind from birth. 2 His

disciples asked him, "Rabbi, who sinned, this man or his parents, that he was born blind?" 3 "Neither this man nor his parents sinned," said Jesus, "but this happened so that the work of God might be displayed in his life. 4 As long as it is day, we must do the work of him who sent me. Night is coming, when no one can work. 5 While I am in the world, I am the light of the world." 6 Having said this, he spit on the ground, made some mud with the saliva, and put it on the man's eyes. 7 "Go," he told him, "wash in the Pool of Siloam" (this word means Sent). So the man went and washed, and came home seeing.

The man was immediately recognized around town as now having sight. People began to talk.

8 His neighbors and those who had formerly seen him begging asked, "Isn't this the same man who used to sit and beg?" 9 Some claimed that he was. Others said, "No, he only looks like him."

But he himself insisted, "I am the man."

10 "How then were your eyes opened?" they asked. 11 He replied, "The man they call Jesus made some mud and put it on my eyes. He told me to go to Siloam and wash. So I went and washed, and then I could see." 12 "Where is this man?" they asked him. "I don't know," he said.

For some reason, miracles needed to be investigated by the religious leaders in power, especially miracles done on the Sabbath. So they had the formerly-blind guy brought before the Pharisees.

15 Therefore the Pharisees also asked him how he had received his sight. "He put mud on my eyes," the man replied, "and I washed, and now I see."

His testimony had immediate impact, forcing the religious leaders to make a spiritual decision.

16 Some of the Pharisees said, "This man is not from God, for he does not keep the Sabbath." But others asked, "How can a sinner perform such signs?" So they were divided.

Many personal stories of an encounter with Jesus are a bit raw and not necessarily theological.

17 Then they turned again to the blind man, "What have you to say about him? It was your eyes he opened." The man replied, "He is a prophet."

I will skip a few verses here. They called the man's parents in to verify that he used to be blind. ("Yep, hasn't seen a thing since birth.") Then they turned their attention back to the now-sighted person who could "see" how silly this line of questioning really was.

24 A second time they summoned the man who had been blind. "Give glory to God by telling the truth," they said. "We know this man is a sinner." 25 He replied, "Whether he is a sinner or not, I don't know. One thing I do know. I was blind but now I see!" 26 Then they asked him, "What did he do to you? How did he open your eyes?" 27 He answered, "I have told you already and you did not listen. Why do you want to hear it again? Do you want to become his disciples too?" 28 Then they hurled insults at him and said, "You are this fellow's disciple! We are disciples of Moses! 29 We know that God spoke to Moses, but as for this fellow, we don't even know where he comes from."

30 The man answered, "Now that is remarkable! You don't know where he comes from, yet he opened my eyes. 31 We know that God does not listen to sinners. He listens to the godly person who does his will. 32 Nobody has ever heard of opening the eyes of a man born blind. 33 If this man were not from God, he could do nothing."

I admit that when I am around people who are a lot smarter than me (which happens in most places), I am intimidated that I will look foolish if I try to talk about what they are talking about. When baseball players talk about baseball, I am on the sidelines. When theologians talk about theology, I am not in the game. But, when I get a chance to tell people that I was a teenaged boy in Richardson, TX who got on a bus that took me to Sunday school where I asked Jesus into my life . . . I can, and will, tell that story to anybody! I'm an expert on my story. We all are.

Notice how powerfully the man in John 9 stood his ground. "You guys may be rich, you may be powerful, you may be smart, but I am telling you what happened to me." The religious leaders had to respond. A faith story is not neutral. When parents tell their faith story to their children, when you tell your story to your students,

THE GOSPEL IS SPOKEN BY A MOUTH THAT HAS BEEN BROUGHT BY FEET TO THE EARS OF ANOTHER PERSON WHO NEEDS TO HEAR IT.

when teenagers tell their stories to other teenagers, a decision has to be made. We may be dismissed like the blind man, but our story is our story and we simply tell what happened when we met Jesus.

To get your students started thinking about their testimonies, help them remember how they came to accept Christ as Savior. Have them think about what they were doing before they heard about Jesus, how they realized their need for Him, and who was helpful in their becoming a Christ-follower. But don't let them stop there.

Your challenge is to help students see that their testimony is not just a past experience, but also a current one. I hope your teenagers have continued to see evidence that God is at work in their lives, guiding and giving on their journey as a disciple. Perhaps God has brought them through a difficult time. Maybe they have been able to use an ability or talent in your church or community. Maybe they have seen other people come to faith in Christ as a result of their story. If so, this can be incorporated into their story as they tell it in the future. See? Our stories aren't static. They grow as God works in and through us.

The most important thing you can help your students do is to simply get started telling their story. Wouldn't it be interesting if you facilitated a time where they could get alone and start writing or typing their story out? Many, if not most, have never done this. Then, make time for students to share what they have written with a friend. Telling their story out loud is the best practice. The more they tell it, the more comfortable they become.

The point we want our students to grasp is simply this: The good news is too good to keep it to ourselves. Before you leave this chapter and move on to the other two strands of discipleship, look at how the telling of a testimony strengthened the church, and glorified God:

> • And with great power the apostles were giving their testimony to the resurrection of the Lord Jesus, and great grace was upon them all. - Acts 4:33 ESV

> • And they have conquered him by the blood of the Lamb and by the word of their testimony, for they loved not their lives even unto death - Revelation 12:11 ESV

In the classic book, *The Lost Art of Disciplemaking*, author Leroy Eims gives these hints about telling our story:

- Make it personal.

- Make it short (deal with essential facts).

- Keep it Christ Centered—what He did is more important than what you or your students did or have done.

- Use the Word of God. Scripture adds power.[4]

Telling our story isn't always easy. But our efforts are never wasted. We can be assured, and we can assure our students, that their efforts in communicating their stories to others are always used by God for His purposes according to His will.

STRAND 4: SHARING THE GOSPEL IN WORD (Evangelism)

In some circles, evangelism has gotten a bad name, hasn't it? Hypocritical personalities, overbearing bullies, and immoral tel-evangelists have given it a bad name. So let's take a breath and regroup before we press forward. Let's remind ourselves that evangelism is simply telling the story of Jesus, and the story of Jesus interacting with us, in such a way that it calls an individual to respond to the incredible gift offered by God. Evangelism is the proclamation, explanation, and/or preaching of the Gospel ("good news") in such a way that a person can understand and make a decision. It is sharing the Gospel in word. (This is an important distinction, as we will see in a few pages.)

One of my favorite passages about evangelism is in Romans. Paul gets pretty fired up about the privilege of telling others about the Gospel:

> As Scripture says, "Anyone who believes in him will never be put to shame." 12 For there is no difference between Jew and Gentile—the same Lord is Lord of all and richly blesses all who call on him, 13 for, "Everyone who calls on the name of the Lord will be saved."14 How, then, can they call on the one they have not believed in? And how can they believe in the one of whom they have not heard? And how can they hear without someone preaching to them? 15 And how can anyone preach unless they are

sent? As it is written: "How beautiful are the feet of those who bring good news!" - Romans 10:11-15

So, the Gospel is spoken by a mouth that has been brought by feet to the ears of another person who needs to hear it. Amen! The Gospel is a spoken message verbally communicated (hopefully) in clear terms. Of course, it can also be written. And if your students share the Gospel through texts, or posts on Instagram, Snapchat, or Twitter, they are most definitely still sharing the Gospel.

The English word "evangelism" comes from the Greek word *euaggelion*. Most literally translated in the noun form, euaggelion means, "gospel" or "good news." In the verb form (euaggelizesthai), the meaning of the word changes slightly to "announce" or "bring good news." The Greek word, in its various forms, appears fifty-five times in the New Testament. In addition to the before-mentioned translations, the Greek word is also translated as "preach."

As you help your students understand the importance of evangelism, it is helpful to show them that sharing the Gospel in word involves three parts: information, conversation, and a call for response. Evangelism includes explaining the activity of God in the redemption of fallen humanity, speaking clearly about sin and its consequences, and calling for the hearer to consider and respond, or repent (to turn from sin and to turn toward God) and believe the Gospel, by faith.

The word for evangelism originally described a reward given to the messenger for bringing the (good) news. Part of my college degree is in marketing, and I am constantly struck by the similarities between what a marketer does and what a disciple does. An advertising person does whatever is needed to get a product or idea in front of an audience who might need it, want it, or buy it. A disciple who takes seriously the role of evangelism does what Paul described in 1 Corinthians 9:22: "To the weak I became weak, that I might win the weak; I have become all things to all men, so that I may by all means save some (NASB)."

As you walk your students toward helping them know feel comfortable sharing the Gospel in words, help them see that a simple question is foundational to the process: "Can they know for sure the spiritual condition of each person in their peer group?" Who among their friends are not Christ-followers? Help students feel the weight of this. As you journey with them, make sure your teenagers grasp the reality of sin, forgiveness, and eternal separation from God. Help plant the seed of empathy in their hearts.

More than anything, this will compel them to reach out to their friends. As an evangelist friend told me once, "nobody ever responded to an invitation to receive Christ that was not given."

Helping students understand the importance of sharing their faith is vital. But helping them have a loose framework for what to say is important as well. It helps me to keep a mental outline when I am sharing the Gospel. I use an old plan called "The Roman Road" which is a series of verses that help me stay on track. You've most likely heard of it. But maybe you haven't.

The verses usually included are Romans 3:23, Romans 6:23, Romans 5:8, Romans 10:13, and Romans 10:9-10.

- For the wages of sin is death, but the gift of God is eternal life in Jesus Christ our Lord. - Romans 6:23

- But God demonstrates His own love toward us, in that while we were yet sinners, Christ died for us. - Romans 5:8

- For whoever calls on the name of the Lord shall be saved. - Romans 10:13

- If you confess with your mouth the Lord Jesus and believe in your heart that God has raised Him from the dead, you will be saved. For with the heart one believes unto righteousness, and with the mouth confession is made unto salvation. - Romans 10:9,10

Personally, I keep the verses in my head because for many people in this generation it seems like you are following a sales script if you use a tract or a pamphlet. As you help lead students to value the act of sharing the Gospel, help them think in terms of natural conversations couched in relationship. Maybe consider modeling a sort of natural, or organic conversation that flows something like this:

If it is OK with you, I would like to share something that is really important to me. Would that be OK? If I say "Romans" something or other, I am talking about the place in the Bible where that verse is found. So here goes. The Bible refers to people who have placed their faith in Jesus Christ as "saved." That means that they have accepted Jesus Christ as their Savior, and will go to heaven when they die. I think that most people in our world think about God and heaven at least some time in their life, and I would like to talk to you about it. I think God is real and I think there is a natural order to things, and I am pretty sure this world is messed up in many ways.

The Bible calls the evil in our world, and the evil things we think and do, "sin." And it also says that everybody sins. Because of our sin, we are separated from God (since He is holy). There are no little or big sins as far as God is concerned, only sin. Romans 6:23 tells me that the penalty for sin is spiritual death, or separation from God, but that price was paid by Jesus Christ. Romans 5:8 tells me that God paid the penalty through the death of His Son Jesus, because He loved us so much. Romans 10:13 tells me that everyone who calls on the name of the Lord (Jesus) will be saved. Romans 10:9-10 tells me that I need to publicly say that Jesus is my Lord, and believe with my heart that God raised Him from the dead. This is important because our faith should not be kept secret. The fact that God has defeated death gives us hope that we can go to heaven when we die. Have you ever accepted Jesus as your Savior and become a disciple? Would you like to do that now?

It's really that simple. Remember, the most important thing you can do is to help your students understand that they do not lead anyone to Christ. God calls whom He calls. And the Spirit is the driving force behind conversion. All we are called to do is faithfully share the Gospel. "Success" and "failure" aren't concepts that have a place in this discussion. Free your students from the burden of "closing the deal." Encourage them to be concerned most with clearly, and earnestly, sharing the good news of Jesus. If the person with whom they share responds positively to the Gospel, encourage students that it's appropriate to lead their friend in a prayer in which they ask Jesus to forgive them of their sins, become their Savior, and help them to live out their life as a disciple. Then, challenge them to get this individual plugged-in to yours or another local church.

STRAND 5: SHARING THE GOSPEL IN DEED
(Social Justice/Compassion)

As we lead students in discipleship, it's important to think about the two ways Scripture talks about how we communicate our faith. We just covered the importance of verbally sharing the Gospel, the "good news" of Jesus. But there is another, equally important, way of sharing the Gospel: through our actions. This is what Jesus called us to in Matthew 5:16:

> In the same way, let your light shine before men, that they may see your good deeds and praise your Father in heaven.

This is what Peter echoed in 1 Peter 2:12:

> Live such good lives among the pagans that, though they accuse you of doing wrong, they may see your good deeds and glorify God on the day he visits us.

This is the heart of James' message in James 2:14-17:

> What good is it, my brothers, if a man claims to have faith but has no deeds? Can such faith save him? Suppose a brother or sister is without clothes and daily food. If one of you says to him, "Go, I wish you well; keep warm and well fed," but does nothing about his physical needs, what good is it? In the same way, faith by itself, if it is not accompanied by action, is dead.

There are other places in Scripture where we see this same concept expressed. As we consider the manner in which we live, our actions communicate a message to the world more often than we may realize. The things we do, and often the things we don't do, tell people about who we are. And if we publicly identify as Christ-followers, our actions have the potential to tell people exactly how much (or how little) Jesus has impacted our lives.

Sharing the Gospel through our actions is a vital part of discipleship. And for this generation of young people, this often takes the form of concern for social justice and/or social compassion issues. Now, this last "strand" may be new to some of you, but probably not to the teenagers in your small groups who are incredibly bent towards social justice. They are probably conservative when it comes to theology (how they think about God), but somewhat liberal when it comes to social issues. A young Rabbi, writing about this generation (the Millennial Generation) and social concern wrote:

> We are a generation overwhelmingly dedicated to social justice. Where there is injustice, we want to respond, whether in-person, online, or through power of the purse -- even when it is that of a teenager who gives what little he can. This impulse can be religiously motivated, much as it has been for me. Yet for many, it is rooted in a fundamental belief in the goodness of people.[5]

He goes on to observe that the Millennials are not rebelling against the social concerns of their parents, but extending them. He affirms the work of another author, Helen Fox, as he observes, "Interestingly, however, she observes a relationship between the attitudes of Millennials and the close relationships they maintain with their parents and those of their parents' generation."[6]

Millennials are concerned with social issues like human trafficking, young women in the sex industry, feeding the homeless, and "sponsoring" children overseas. They often sign up for such sponsorships at camps or conferences. One concern I have is that social justice would be reduced to a fad, represented only by a short-term mission trip or sponsored child (sometimes committing their parents to a long term financial arrangement), and not as an essential part of discipleship. But my concerns aside, the point remains: your teenagers are squarely in the middle of a cultural context where social justice is seen as a worthy cause.

Influential writer and pastor John Stott, who died in 2011 at the age of 90, was ahead of his time in connecting real discipleship with real concern for persons who needed tangible help, in addition to the message of the Gospel. He wrote a commentary on the Sermon the Mount, originally titled, "Christian Counterculture," with a primary theme of interpreting the words of Jesus as a challenge to be involved in ministry to the physical, emotional, and financial hurt in the world outside the church. Jesus' familiar words to the first generation of disciples gathered on the Galilean hillside were,

> "You are the salt of the earth. But if the salt loses its saltiness, how can it be made salty again? It is no longer good for anything, except to be thrown out and trampled by men. "You are the light of the world. A city on a hill cannot be hidden. Neither do people light a lamp and put it under a bowl. Instead they put it on its stand, and it gives light to everyone in the house. In the same way, let your light shine before men, that they may see your good deeds and praise your Father in heaven. "Do not think that I have come to abolish the Law or the Prophets; I have not come to abolish them but to fulfill them. – Matthew 5:13-17

Stott wrote, "If the beatitudes describe the essential character of the disciples of Jesus, the salt and light metaphors indicate their influence for good in the world."[7] His last book, published only a year before he died, was entitled *The Radical Disciple*, which summarized Stott's lifetime challenge for the church to be engaged in culture. In the 1970's, Stott was a voice for real disciples, individually and collectively as the church, to be involved in social and political issues.[8]

Another valid concern for disciplemakers is that social justice is reduced to what was known in the 20th century as "the Social Gospel." If you want the whole backstory, do an internet search. But to make a long story short, the social Gospel was a movement that called the church to be concerned with social problems like the widening gap between rich and poor, alcoholism, crime, racism, environmental concerns, and urban blight. Many critics of the social Gospel, like famous preacher Dwight Moody, claimed that concentrating on social justice took the focus away from evangelism.

But I do not think this is the primary way your students understand social justice. I think for most of our teenagers, it is an authentic expression of their love for Christ. Of all of the five strands, this is the one that is probably easiest to cultivate in your students. As much as anything, your task is simply to authorize the work they are already doing. Provide opportunities for them to continue to serve others. Help them connect the dots between the causes they are passionate about, and the potential evangelistic nature of their involvement in them.

As I write this, my church in New Orleans is very involved in social justice issues. I probably should have confessed that the emphasis on social action in a hurting city like New Orleans was one of the main reasons I would elevate social justice to a major pillar in discipleship. My pastor wrote an article that brilliantly summarizes why social justice does not take away from evangelism, but stands alongside it. I have excerpted a portion of his article with permission. In the article, Pastor Crosby described the "Care Effect" (what we call the social ministries of FBC New Orleans). He wrote what I wish you and your students would grasp about the connection between social justice and the Gospel.[9]

> The Care Effect ministries of First Baptist New Orleans are a product of and a manifestation of the Gospel of Jesus Christ. But they are not an illustration of the social Gospel.
>
> These ministries are an effort to mimic the life and work of Jesus of Nazareth, who was powerful in "word and deed"

(Luke 24:19), and to follow the instructions of Scripture in devoting ourselves to a life of "love and good deeds" (Hebrews 10:24).

Many Southern Baptist churches—and evangelical congregations in general—have abandoned any serious effort to address obvious needs among widows, orphans, and the poor. The commands of Scripture regarding the needy have been viewed as incumbent on the individual Christian rather than the church as a body. The churches have organized themselves for evangelism and discipleship around the Great Commission (Matthew 28:180-20), rather than love of neighbor as ordered in the Great Commandment (Matthew 22:36-40).

Where is the plan for our churches to be organized to accomplish the Great Commandment? How will such a plan become part of the DNA of our churches?

Our preference for organizing to do the Great Commission, rather than the Great Commandment, looks and sounds self-serving to many people both within and outside of the churches. Absent the Gospel proclamation embodied in deeds of compassion, we seem to be vigorously recruiting new members because we need more bodies and money to count.

This lopsided presentation of the Gospel and of the Savior—a Great Commission without a Great Commandment—is undercutting evangelism and discipleship. It doesn't look or sound true because it is not true to Jesus Himself, or the Gospel he came to incarnate and proclaim.

We have a Savior whose works of compassion are beyond famous. Loving deeds permeate the popular perceptions of Jesus because they permeated the person and work of Jesus. These deeds of compassion are imbedded in the languages of the earth through references to the Good Samaritan, the lost sheep, the prodigal son, the Beatitudes, etc. No presentation of the Savior is complete without them.

Words are not enough. Absent the deeds, they will not satisfy this new generation no matter how powerful the apologetic may be. Words have never been enough. That is why God became flesh.

We need a theory and practice of church and Sunday School that includes the Great Commandment. Fulfilling the Great Commandment should be in our budget, in our staff assignments, and on our weekly church calendar. Our Southern Baptist churches need to be famous for love and good deeds.

Then we will look and sound much more like our winsome, wonderful Savior.

Obviously my pastor was writing from within his context as a leader of a Southern Baptist Church. But I am willing to bet that no matter your denominational affiliation, you probably see shades of truth in his words. I think the heart of this message is one worth passing along to your students. I believe social justice/social compassion is a pillar of discipleship, one that may very well build a more effective evangelical bridge into our world than our words.

IT SHOULD GO WITHOUT SAYING, BUT I WILL SAY IT ANYWAY

As I finish up this chapter, I have just finished reading *Jesus-Centered Youth Ministry* by Rick Lawrence. As I look back on what I have written in this chapter, I believe in it with all my heart. I believe there are things that we value (the DNA strands), and I believe there are things we do in response to the work of God in our lives (spiritual disciplines will be discussed in the next chapter). But Rick has a reminder in the first chapter of his book that is so insightful that I have to mention it.

Using the old story about pigs, chickens, and commitment (you've heard this one: a chicken makes a contribution to a bacon and egg breakfast, but a pig is "all in"), Lawrence says:

> I believe youth ministries, and churches in general, have been using a flawed strategy for discipleship that produces chickens, not pigs. I call it the "understand and apply" strategy. It assumes people grow deeper in their faith when they understand biblical principles and apply them to their lives.[10]

Even though I believe in spiritual disciplines, and I am committed to the valued components of discipleship, I have to affirm what Rick is saying. Our activity can sometimes get in the way of a love affair with Jesus. I have been married for over 30 years as I write this. I love Judi with all that I am. I would not expect to be able to replace the, "I'm just crazy about you after all these years" with actions that try to prove my love. She likes flowers, and she loves it when I wash the dishes. But the core of my relationship with Judi is that I cannot imagine being without her.

Lawrence cites the response of Peter in John 6 when many were deserting Jesus as disciples, and Jesus asked the twelve if they were hitting the road as well. Peter answered and said, "Lord, to whom shall we go? You have words of eternal life." (John 6:69, NASB). The paraphrase of Peter's response that Rick uses is, "I don't understand a lot of what you're saying and I can't comprehend the things you do, but I know I have nowhere else to go. You've ruined me for you."[11]

As adults who are privileged to be in students' lives, we should examine the discipleship relationship we have with Jesus. Are we ruined without Him? Are we trying to check off a discipleship checklist with all the things we do? I am thankful to Rick for a gut check that reminds me to *be*.

WHAT ABOUT YOU?

1. Before we can teach teenagers to have a passion for knowing God's Word, we have to have a passion for it ourselves. What is keeping you from having a passion for God's Word?

2. How old are you? 25? 55? Could you write one Bible verse from memory, reference and all, for every year you've been alive? If this became a goal for you, what impact do you think it would have on your faith?

3. Part of being able to tell your story is to have spent time thinking about it. Try this exercise: Write what your life was like before Jesus, a description of your decision to come to faith in Jesus, and the difference Jesus has made in your life since coming to faith in Him. Really. Actually write this down. You'll be surprised how writing it will help you organize your thoughts more effectively.

4. What are you doing in your disciplemaking efforts to help teenagers more effectively share the Gospel through words? How are you helping them knock down some of the barriers that keep them from sharing their faith?

WE MUST DESIRE TO DRAW CLOSER TO GOD THROUGH OUR ACTIONS, BUT OUR ACTIONS DO NOT MAKE US ANY MORE SAVED, OR GIVE US ANY ADDITIONAL GRACE.

CHAPTER 4
THE DISCIPLINES OF DISCIPLESHIP

Dallas Willard, one of the most influential voices in the area of spiritual formation, had a concept he called the "Golden Triangle" of spiritual transformation.[1] The three sides of the triangle are:

1. The faithful acceptance of everyday problems.

2. Interaction with God's Spirit, opening up to the work that only the Holy Spirit can do in us.

3. The aspect of discipleship that involves spiritual activities, i.e., the stuff we do.

Willard used the common term "spiritual disciplines" to refer to these spiritual activities. This third side of the triangle is what this chapter is about.

The word "discipline" brings to mind all kinds of things, most of them negative or painful. The discipline of training for a triathlon earns long hours in the pool, on the road, and riding a bicycle. The discipline of losing weight means that your diet only allows you to eat foods you hate (but you can eat a lot of those), while telling you to stay away from anything that resembles comfort food. The discipline of time management means working when you really don't want to work, studying when you really don't want to study, and turning off the television (computer, phone, game console, etc.) when you are wasting time instead of giving your body needed sleep.

And yet, no discussion of discipleship can be complete without a focus on spiritual disciplines. Think of your favorite athletes. They train for hours each day to build up strength, speed, stamina, and skill to be as good as they can be. Nurses spend years in school and in practice, developing patient skills, and learning about all of the medicines the human body needs when it isn't working right. Computer programmers have the patient discipline of writing code until the program does exactly what it is intended to do.

A spiritual discipline is a habit that keeps you open to what God is about in your life and in the world. Spiritual disciplines (like any discipline) are the workout exercises that develop us spiritually.

Spiritual disciplines exercise our spirit, mind, will, and emotions so that we become more devoted to God. The more we practice these disciplines, the more they become habits. And the more they become habits, the stronger our faith becomes. Ralph Waldo Emerson said,

> "Sow a thought and you reap an action; sow an act and you reap a habit; sow a habit and you reap a character; sow a character and you reap a destiny."[2]

When spiritual disciplines are the workout routine of our life as a follower of Christ, our thoughts move to Him, our actions reflect His ways, and our character imitates His. Now, we have to be careful: we cannot work our way to Christ-likeness. But the amazing thing is that our engagement in spiritual disciplines tills the soil of our hearts so that the Holy Spirit finds fertile soil prepared for seed. Spiritual disciplines align us, and our students, with the work the Spirit is already doing in our lives. Spiritual discipline is our way of partnering with the Spirit on the sanctification journey.

And yet, it isn't always easy, for our students or for us. Consider the perspective of the writer of Hebrews as he counseled the people who were weary in their faith:

> No discipline seems pleasant at the time, but painful. Later on, however, it produces a harvest of righteousness and peace for those who have been trained by it.
> - Hebrews 12:11

I became a recreational runner in my late 30's because I wanted to justify my love for eating. I ran a bunch of half-marathons and a couple of full marathons. As I got close to the date for one of the runs, I realized that I was running between 35 and 40 miles per week! If I had started my training for a run by going out and running that kind of mileage, I would have never made it. In fact, I would have most likely injured myself.

Discipline is starting with small steps and moving to a place where we have a sustainable habit. The discipline of running around the block was painful at first. As I trained, the miles piled up and the completion of the New York Marathon was a sweet, rewarding feeling at the other end.

One of my friends competes in marathons and triathlons. If I continue to use the illustration of training to talk about the disciplines of discipleship, I think that a triathlon is a better example. I have no personal experience as a triathlete, so I am just observing. But training for a running event is one-dimensional. You run. Training for a running/biking/swimming event requires preparation in all three areas.

It is time for me to leave the athletic illustrations before I embarrass myself. As we connect the dots between physical and spiritual training, consider what Paul said in 1 Timothy 4:7-8:

> Discipline yourself for the purpose of godliness; for bodily discipline is only of little profit, but godliness is profitable for all things, since it holds promise for the present life and also for the life to come. (NASB)

As we begin to think about what it means to lead students to a greater investment in spiritual disciplines, let's remember the goal of what we're asking them to do. Spiritual training involves intentional activities that aim toward a goal: maturity. Before I get into specific disciplines, allow me to express a warning. As you lead teenagers to a deeper understanding of the actions of a disciple, don't let the "discipline for the purpose of godliness" become a legalistic "check-the-box" kind of duty. I hope that the purpose of spiritual discipline is to learn and grow in intimacy with Jesus. Donald Whitney, another excellent author who writes a lot about spiritual development, said, "Discipline without direction is drudgery."[3] We have to have a goal. And that goal is Christ-likeness. In the excellent book, *Sticky Faith*, Kara Powell and Chap Clark penned this great sentence: "Spiritual disciplines do not make us righteous because we do them, but rather they put us in a position to be drawn into trusting Christ more fully."[4] This is the heart of what we need to communicate to our students about spiritual disciplines. We must desire to draw closer to God through our actions, but our actions do not make us any more saved, or give us any additional grace.

As much as anything in this book, this isn't simply a chapter for teenagers. You simply must be endeavoring to live these disciplines in your own life as you seek to lead students to do the same. Let us dive in to an examination of some of the basic disciplines, as well as a drive-by view of some of the ancillary ones. As with everything in this book, my hope is that you pick up something for yourself and for your students.

A FEW OF THE DISCIPLINES

Engaging With God's Word

Since we talked about Scripture memory and understanding the Bible as a grand narrative in the last chapter, I won't start over here. But please don't diminish its importance. In talking about DNA, I wrote a lot about hearing, reading, studying, memorizing, meditating, and obeying God's Word. I would say again, this is God's most complete way of making Himself known to us, His children. It is vital that we help teenagers build this discipline in their lives. And yet, for many youth workers, this is one of the biggest challenges they face. Many youth workers ask what they can do to get teenagers reading the Bible more. I think we may be asking the question all wrong.

I think the better question may be, "What can we do to help teenagers value God more?" God must be important to our teenagers, specifically the idea of knowing God. When knowing God is important, when being close to Him matters to teenagers, the act of reading the Bible simply becomes the means by which they come to know Him. If they value God, they will value reading the Bible. Which leads me to the next point . . .

We also must be careful not to be solely focused on the methodology of engaging with the Bible. While it is definitely true that teenagers need guidance in how and what to study, we have to change the way we teach teenagers to think about the Bible. We've forgotten that reading the Bible is relational. We should strive to teach teenagers that the Bible is first-and-foremost a heart-driven, deeply personal, experiential encounter with God. We go to the Bible to engage with God, to meet God. We have to stop putting technique and behavior first, and make Bible reading about feeding our relationship with God.

One of the best ways to get students to build the discipline of engaging with God's Word is to keep our approaches fresh. Get creative with how you lead students to interact with Scripture. This includes, but certainly is not limited to,

- Praying through the Psalms as personal worship.

- Choosing a specific attribute of God, reading about it in Scripture, and meditating on it over the course of a few days.

- Learning some of the different names used for God and choosing to pray to Him using a name that speaks to them personally.

- Creating something, anything, using Scripture.

These are just a few of the many different ways to lead teenagers to engage with Scripture. They represent a varied approach to encountering God in His Word, and help students to break free from one specific way of looking at the Bible.

Finally, one of the most valuable ways we can help teenagers begin to embrace this discipline is by modeling a passion for God's Word. A love for God's Word is caught, not taught. Your students will pick up on whether or not you value the Bible. If you model a passion for meeting God in His Word, your students will pick up on it.

Prayer

Some people believe that prayer is like sitting on Santa's lap at the mall, asking for presents. Some people believe that prayer is the magic potion or incantation required to cause God to spring into action. I hope that you and your students increasingly realize that prayer is a conversation with God. Prayer has been around forever–when Adam walked in the Garden of Eden, talking with God, that was prayer.

Prayer should be more conversation than a one-way speech. We talk with God, expressing worship, confessing our sins, asking, and receiving. We talk with God, making our requests known to Him in faith, according to His will. We seek and find, asking for God to reveal His will. We talk and listen, a two way exchange with someone who loves us. Prayer is the language of our relationship with God.

My favorite definition of prayer is by Rosalind Rinker in her book *Prayer: Conversing With God*. In it she writes, "Prayer is a dialogue between two persons who love each other."[5] Georgia Harkness wrote that, "Prayer is not overcoming God's reluctance, but laying hold of God's willingness."[6] It is definitions like these that should compel us to think differently about how we talk about prayer with our teenagers.

So how do we teach teenagers to pray as a discipline? Many students learn from their parents or grandparents. Some students who do not have family members to teach or model prayer learn from other Christians. It makes a difference when, at a meal, we sincerely offer thanks. It makes a difference when we acknowledge that someone is having a hard time and stop then and there to pray for them. Aloud. It makes a difference when, in Bible study, we identify a psalm as a prayer. It makes a difference when we study it and connect the psalmists cry of thankfulness or repentance or worship with our own.

The Internet is full of suggestions and tips for different models or types of prayers. You can search for creative prayer activities and find plenty of them. Again, I would suggest that you do. And I would suggest that you implement them with your students. But more than anything, I suggest that you teach your students about the importance of prayer, that you model prayer for them, and that you constantly remind them that you are praying for them. Showing them that prayer is important to you will go a long way toward helping them build positive attitudes about prayer, which in turn will play a big role in their success at building a solid prayer habit.

I think it's also healthy to be transparent about the challenges of prayer. We all have reasons why prayer seems to be out of reach. We don't have time. We don't know how. God never seems to listen. We're not sure that it "works." We get distracted. Everyone has times when prayer doesn't feel right. Tiredness, bitterness, apathy, and despair can come between our Father and us. The words aren't there, and so our prayers stop, sometimes for only a short period of time, sometimes for good.

Remember that all discipline is painful in the short term. Like a runner who works through a cramp, or goes to physical therapy to help heal a pulled muscle, we keep our eyes on the return to the discipline even if we have neglected it for a season. Help your students understand this and you will go a long way toward helping them live out the actions of discipleship.

Silence and Solitude
In our busy, noisy world we need to "unplug" and get away in order to be alone, and be ourselves with our Lord. We usually call it a "quiet time," which involves some devotional study accompanied by prayer. In addition to a regular devotion, a disciple needs periodic times to "go off the grid." You might not have considered silence (or solitude) as something a disciple does. Ideally, silence and solitude help followers of Christ learn to interact more deeply

with the Lord. Silence is a discipline that creates margins, un-scripted time for God to confirm or redirect our journey by speaking in us, and through us, as we related to Him and to others. (We also must recognize that for our teenagers, this may very well be one of the most countercultural practices for them.)

The normal way to practice solitude and silence is get alone with God to be still and know (Psalm 46:10) in a quiet place for some time. Maybe you encourage your students to go to a park, or nature trail, or to a spot in the woods. Maybe you challenge them to find a special room or chair at home, though at home they may quickly be challenged with things they should be doing. Wherever you encourage them to go, make sure that they take only a Bible, notebook, and pen (if anything at all). Be sure they understand that their i-things are to be turned off.

Dallas Willard is one of my favorite writers. Have I mentioned that? He had this to say about solitude, silence, and Sabbath:

> Solitude well practiced will break the power of busyness, haste, isolation, and loneliness. You will see that the world is not on you shoulders after all. You will find yourself, and God will find you in new ways. Joy and peace will begin to bubble up within you, and arrive from things and events around you. Praise and prayer will come to you, and from within you. The soul anchor established in solitude will remain solid when you return to your ordinary life with others.

> Silence means quietness, freedom from sounds except natural ones like breathing, bird songs, and wind and water moving. It also means not talking. Silence completes solitude, for without it you cannot be alone. You remain subject to the pulls and pushes of a world that exhaust you and keep you in bondage, distracting you from God and your own soul.[7]

So, really. Let's think for a second about how this will be received by your students. There is a good chance they'll look at you like you're a tree-hugging weirdo. In the world your students live in, there is virtually zero cultural value placed on silence and solitude. In fact, you may say that the opposite is true: culture values networks of people and noise, noise, noise.

But over and over again, Jesus modeled this practice for us. And the Church through the centuries has held on to this as a core component of growing spiritually. Just because it is countercultural to our students does not mean we should cede this practice to culture. As Christ-followers we are by nature called to be revolutionary. This is one discipline you should fight for. Do what you can to challenge your students to embrace this discipline.

Fasting

Fasting is the discipline of doing without for the purpose of focusing on God and His ways. Our students' routines of eating, drinking, sleeping, working, playing, and doing all manner of things with electronic devices are well established. As creatures of habit, they settle into a rhythm of life, and sometimes just drift through days as if someone has pushed the "play" button. In many ways, our students, and us, are robotically reacting to the demands of the day.

Fasting means that we shake up the schedule. We do without food, or something else, for a couple of reasons. First, we shake up the routine so that we will feel out of sync enough to remind us to seek God. We may be looking for direction in a decision, confidence in a conversation, or repair in a relationship. Second, we become more aware of our dependence because we are reminded that God provides everything that we voluntarily do without.

When I think about fasting as a spiritual discipline, I usually (agonizingly) think about how hungry I am about to be. My hunch is this may be true for your students as well. I do not necessarily like change, and when I am out of my routine it can be distressing. Yet in our distress at being out of rhythm, we might be more aware of who God is.

I saw something on Charles Stanley's website once that stuck with me. He said, "Fasting involves a strong desire to hear from God, a period of time to connect with Him, and a willingness to abstain from food or some activity . . . so that we might draw closer to God and receive His encouragement and direction."[8] The practice of fasting reminds us of how selfish we can be. It is self-denial, but also an honest assessment of how much we desire other things than God's best.

Some of your students may very well respond to the idea of fasting with a little bit of a sideways glance. After all, it does sound pretty antiquated. But the truth is that Jesus expected His disciples to fast. He fasted. And He expects us to fast. Jesus talks about fasting in the same sentence as prayer, suggesting that fasting is of equal importance. Jesus fasted for 40 days in the wilderness before He begin to minister on earth. He gave specific instructions for how to fast (Matthew 9:15, Matthew 6:16-18). The early church fasted to hear from God (Acts 13:2-3), to seek God's protection and provision on those who led them, and on those whom they sent out on mission (Acts 14:23). The disciples were instructed that certain spiritual challenges needed to be met with prayer and fasting (Mark 9:29).

Maybe your students will resonate most soundly with a fast that does not involve food at all. Maybe they would be more aware of God and their need for Him if they were to fast from media, or technology. Fasting is not just about what goes in our stomach, but also what goes in our mind. I have always been intrigued by Psalm 101:1-3. The Psalmist is worshiping and realizes that God and God's way must take precedence over other things:

> I will sing of your love and justice; to you, O LORD, I will sing praise. I will be careful to lead a blameless life—when will you come to me? I will walk in my house with blameless heart. I will set before my eyes no vile thing. The deeds of faithless men I hate; they will not cling to me.

Our praise to God for His love and justice, our determination to walk in integrity, and our perspective on good and evil occasionally need to be brought into focus by a purposeful refusal to let our eyes dwell on worthless things. Does this suggest a media fast? Could going off grid from television, radio, e-mail, and social networking have the effect of redirecting your students' attention to the blameless way? I think it could. And though it might be a tough sell for some of your students at first, once they experience, it may very well become something they crave.

OTHER SPIRITUAL DISCIPLINES

The spiritual disciplines we just discussed may be considered the "biggies." Chances are you have heard of each of them before, and hopefully, are even implementing them to some degree in your ministry. But there are more spiritual disciplines to consider, especially as you seek to lead students toward a well-rounded followership of Jesus.

Dallas Willard, in *The Spirit of the Disciplines*,[9] and Richard Foster, in *Celebration of Discipline*,[10] have compiled a list of spiritual disciplines and practices they believe were modeled by Christ. These two lists may or may not be exhaustive. But, I think you will agree with me that they represent a wonderful framework for thinking about your disciplemaking efforts. These disciplines are typically organized into two categories: the disciplines of abstinence (or "letting go"), and the disciplines of activity.

Disciplines of Letting Go

These practices allow us to relinquish something in order to gain something new. We abstain from "busy-ness" in ministry, family life, and work. We stop talking for a while to hear from God. We give up buying another material possession to experience God more fully. First Peter 2:11 warns us to "abstain from sinful desires, which war against your soul." Identify what is keeping you from experiencing greater strength and perspective. Do you talk too much? Are possessions controlling you? Are you too worried about what others think? Choose disciplines that will help you become more dependent on God. We've already covered silence, solitude, and fasting, disciples both of these authors valued. Here are a few more disciplines:

- *Frugality*—Learning to live with less money and still meet your basic needs. Before buying something new, choose to go without, or pick a less expensive alternative that will serve your basic needs. Live a simple, focused life.

- *Chastity*—For a married couple, this might be voluntarily choosing to abstain from sexual pleasures for a time (those pleasures that are deemed morally right in the bond of marriage) to find higher fulfillment in God. But for teenagers, this could include an emphasis not only on sexual purity in regards to sexual intercourse and sexual activity, but also an increased focus on the purity of their thoughts, and the type of media they consume.

- *Secrecy*—This discipline is all about avoiding self-promotion and serving God without others knowing. It's giving in secret. I think teenagers will find this one to be a pretty contagious discipline. Challenge students to serve "behind the scenes" in a ministry that they are assured few will know about.

- *Sacrifice*—Giving of our resources beyond what seems reasonable to remind us of our dependence on Christ. This discipline may be one of the most foreign disciplines for many of your students, depending on the social context in which you're teaching. Encouraging students to give their time or finances to the Lord beyond what they normally would is a powerful tool to shape their characters.

Disciplines of Activity

Dallas Willard writes, "The disciplines of abstinence must be counter-balanced and supplemented by disciplines of engagement (activity)." It's choosing to participate in activities that nurture our souls and strengthen us for the race ahead. We've already covered Bible study and prayer. But Willard mentions a few more disciplines, such as:

- *Worship*—Offering praise and adoration to God. His praise should continually be on our lips and in our thoughts. Lead your students to read psalms, hymns, or spiritual songs, or sing to the Lord daily utilizing their favorite praise songs. Encourage students to keep praise ever before them as they think of God's mighty deeds in their lives.

- *Fellowship*—Mutual caring and ministry in the body of Christ. Youth group isn't just hanging out with friends. Remind your students that they should meet regularly with one another to find ways to minister to others. Their time together should be fun, encouraging, transformative, and centered on Christ.

- *Confession*—Regularly confess your sins to the Lord and other trusted individuals. This is an important discipline, but is tricky with teenagers. Make sure you have solid boundaries set between you and them, and between them and their friends. Trust is key.

- *Submission*—Leading teenagers to humble themselves before God and others while seeking accountability in relationships. Helping students find faithful brothers or sisters in Christ who can lovingly hold them accountable for their actions and growth in Christ is challenging. But it can be done. And when it works, it's powerful.

We've reached the end of our discussion on spiritual disciplines. I hope you have plenty of ammunition to begin thinking about how you might implement some of these practices in your disciplemaking strategy.

Spiritual disciplines won't always "take" with your students, especially not on the first try. It takes time and intentionality to help lead students to embrace these practices. But they are a vital part of what it means to truly follow Christ. Stay the course. Encourage. Be patient. Partner with parents. Trust the Spirit to work amazing transformation in your students' lives.

And most of all, enjoy the ride.

WHAT ABOUT YOU?

1. Which spiritual discipline have you had relative success practicing in your life? What difference has this made in your relationship with Christ?

2. Be honest: Which discipline is the most difficult for you? Can you think why this might be the case?

3. If you were to focus on one or two spiritual disciplines that have traditionally been tough for you to put into practice, how do you think your faith-life might be enriched? What impact might it have on the teenagers you disciple?

4. Here's a challenge: Get with your team, or a ministry mentor, and take a shot at coming up with a plan to lead your students to implement some of these spiritual disciplines in their lives.

CHAPTER 5
DISCIPLESHIP AT HOME AND CHURCH

One of my favorite stories in Scripture is when Joseph and Mary took Jesus to the Temple in Jerusalem when he was 12 years old. At the end of the Passover celebration, the family headed home. Tradition tells us that the women and children headed out early, while the men finished packing for the journey. The idea was that the men would catch up with the slower group by evening.

Apparently, Mary headed out thinking Jesus would be with Joseph and the men. Joseph assumed Jesus was with His mother. At the end of a long day's journey, they discovered Jesus was not with either one of them, or their relatives, or their friends. I imagine that was one long night, punctuated by angry words, long silences, soft weeping, and restless sleep. Early the next morning, they started an equally long journey back to Jerusalem for another night of anxious worry.

I believe that Mary and Joseph were candidates for the best parents to have ever lived. After all, God trusted his only Son to their care. We know they were virtuous, spiritually aware, and obedient to the Spirit's leading. It encourages me that even the best parents sometimes miscommunicate, worry about their children, and occasionally forget to pick up their kid up at church. It is a classic scene, when a frantic, stressed Jewish mother finally finds her preteen son:

> "Son, why have you treated us like this? Your father and I have been anxiously searching for you." "Why were you searching for me?" he asked. "Didn't you know I had to be in my Father's house?" But they did not understand what he was saying to them. - Luke 2:48-50

Don't you love it! Mary calls him "son," not "Jesus," "honey," or "sweetheart." I think it was the New Testament equivalent to when my mother called me by my first, middle, and last name. "You treated us . . ." She took it personally, she blamed the child, and she imagined it was intentional. "Anxiously searching . . ." That's a biblical understatement! If you put yourself in their shoes, you can feel the raging and conflicted emotions. Mary and Joseph were just like every other parent would be in a similar situation.

Jesus, the perfect and sinless Son of God, responds to His mother. The tone is hard to distinguish; it certainly could be said many ways. But, it was not said to dishonor them. Note that Jesus does not blame His parents, does not hint that it was intentional, and despite having spent two nights on His own, does not seem to be anxious at all. "Didn't you know I had to be in my Father's house?" In other words, "I'm right where you left me," or "I stayed in the safest place I could find," or "I am where you taught me that I belong."

And then the best insight into parenting teenagers in the entire Bible: "they did not understand what he was saying." The best parents God could find sometimes did not understand their teenager. I have a PhD and decades of youth ministry experience, and I have often not understood my own children. And so although I believe parents know their teenagers better than anyone, I also suspect there are times when they too are confounded, anxious, emotionally conflicted, and uncertain. In fact, I know there are.

This important story sets the tone for this chapter. Why? Two reasons. First, Scripture is clear that God's primary plan for discipling teenagers is the family unit first, and by implication, the church body second. We'll get to this in just a moment.

But the second reason this story is beneficial is fairly obvious: the teenage years may very well be some of the most taxing on the parent-child relationship. To quote the noted 20th century scholar, The Fresh Prince, aka Will Smith, "Parents just don't understand" (or at least that's how it appears to their teenagers). So many factors contribute to this: hormonal changes, personality changes, identity formation, peer pressure, increased autonomy leading to increased exposure to negative cultural elements, and so on. There are certain relational barriers that often arise during this season. I think this story is particularly important to us because parents often struggle in discipling their own children, even though they want their children to be spiritually strong, hold firmly to the things they value most, and make wise decisions with their lives. And so, while any book on discipleship worth its salt must uphold the model of family-based discipleship, youth ministers play a vital role in disciplemaking.

This chapter will focus on the importance of disciplemaking happening both in the home and at church. But it will put extra emphasis on the home. We've already talked in detail about your role as a youth worker. I don't want to have finished the book and not spent time talking about what discipleship looks like in the home. How you will implement this knowledge in your disciplemaking strategy is up to you.

This is not a prescribed, step-by-step plan. I don't know your specific ministry context or structure. And with what I hope will be a wide range of individuals reading this book, if I prescribed a program, or plan, I would miss as many youth ministers as I would hit. Instead, I am going to paint as clear a picture of family-based discipleship as I can paint. You will be armed with at least some of what you need to know to allow this to influence your disciplemaking. I encourage you to soak this information in and then begin to ask questions about how your youth ministry can take partner with parents to support the discipleship that is happening in their homes.

DISCIPLESHIP AT HOME IS GOD'S PLAN

God designed the home to be the primary place for learning the life of faith. Both the Old and New Testaments give us direct support for putting the parent-child relationship at the center of the disciple-making process.

> These commandments that I give you today are to be upon your hearts. Impress them on your children. Talk about them when you sit at home and when you walk along the road, when you lie down and when you get up.
> – Deuteronomy 6:6-7

> Fathers, do not exasperate your children; instead, bring them up in the training and instruction of the Lord.
> – Ephesians 6:4

There are numerous other Scriptural examples that have the same general message. The church has an important role in discipleship, but the home is the place where faith can be expressed continually and consistently. God's plan is for Christian mothers and fathers to model faith, talk about faith, teach faith, and discipline children in the faith. The most significant human relationships are the bedrock for the most significant discipleship.

Before I move forward, we ought to recognize that many parents may not have grown up in a Christian home, or perhaps it was "Christian" by tradition, but not in a truly tangible way. Many parents feel inadequate or incapable because of this. But the truth is that many parents who did grow up in Christian homes are also in the process of learning how to be disciplemaking parents for the first time.

Many Christian parents did not have discipleship modeled for them. We have to show great empathy as youth workers. Our first inclination can't be to look down our noses because we don't perceive discipleship happening in some of our Christian homes. This truth–that discipleship in the home is God's plan–is sometimes a source of frustration for parents. But it shouldn't be. It should be a source of hope. One of the ways we should live out our role as disciplemaker is through encouraging parents. You have the chance to remind them that whatever effort they make as a parent to develop their child's faith is an effort supported by God Himself. We need to show parents we are on their side.

Discipleship at Home Is Fruitful

The second reason discipleship must be intentional in the home is that it benefits teenagers.

> Children, obey your parents in the Lord, for this is right. "Honor your father and mother"—which is the first commandment with a promise—"that it may go well with you and that you may enjoy long life on the earth. – Ephesians 6:1-3

I love that Paul says the fruit of a parent's discipleship effort is that life will "go well" for those who follow instruction. There is reward to be reaped in this life, and the next, when parents walk wisely.

Now, the reality is that many times teenagers may seem to walk away from that blessing. Many parents will experience dark days when they have to cling tightly to Proverbs 22:6, "Train a child in the way he should go, and when he is old he will not turn from it." We share this pain. Watching a student waiver from his or her "first love" is painful. But God promises hope for Christian parents, even in days when rebellion and rejection are all they can see. The hope they have, and that we share, is that what was planted in the teenager's heart will eventually (and ultimately) be the source of blessing.

Here are two truths that seem to be contradictory, but really are two sides of the same coin when it comes to disciplemaking:

- *Discipleship is evident* – One of the great joys of parenting, and of youth ministry, is that we can actually see teenagers grow up and mature. Part of it is visible in physical changes, as they grow taller and broader, becoming young men and young women. But part of it is also visible in the way they take on responsibility, the way they talk about spiritual issues, and the way they choose to act. So much happens in the short period of time we call adolescence that it is obvious. Luke 2:52 says, "Jesus grew in wisdom and in stature, and in favor with God and man." His growth was evident.

- *Discipleship is invisible* - Another wonderful joy in disciplemaking is knowing that not everything teenagers have learned is evident; much is invisible. When Jesus said, "didn't you know" in the story we opened this chapter with, I think He had learned something from Mary and Joseph that they did not know He had learned. We partner with parents to plant seeds in the soil of teenager's lives. We water them alongside the parents, but we often do not see how those seeds are growing until they spring up almost unexpectedly. Another way that discipleship is invisible is that parents and youth workers alike aren't always aware that we are planting seeds. Teenagers are always watching, always listening, and always learning, whether we are intending to teach or not. The final way discipleship is invisible is that much of what Christ has done in us will not be revealed until He returns (Romans 8:18)!

Discipleship at Home Requires Intimacy

Intimacy is revealing ourselves in personal, deep, and transparent ways. This intimacy is frightening for some parents. Ever since the Garden of Eden, when Adam and Eve went from being naked and not ashamed (Gen 2:25), to hiding from the Lord in shame (Gen 3:8), one of the biggest challenges for people is to reveal our own faults and struggles with others. This is most pronounced when parents want to create spiritual intimacy in the home; when they want to pray with their spouse, or child, or lead the family in devotions.

I STRONGLY BELIEVE THAT THE CHURCH SHOULD NOT REPLACE THE FAMILY. BUT I ALSO BELIEVE THE FAMILY NEEDS THE CHURCH.

I have given them the glory that you gave me, that they may be one as we are one: I in them and you in me. May they be brought to complete unity to let the world know that you sent me and have loved them even as you have loved me. – John 17:22-23

Jesus' description of a disciple's relationship with God in John 17 has the same tone as the "one flesh" idea in the husband-wife relationship. We often think of the physical, or sexual, when we consider "one flesh." But there is much more to it than that. Spiritual leadership in the home calls for transparency and vulnerability. Meaningful disciplemaking, both at home and at church, calls for talking about personal doubts, and fears, and questions with teenagers. When parents open their spiritual lives (warts and all) to their teens, they show how faith is truly at work. They make it okay to raise questions, or even have doubts, without being a "bad Christian," or worse.

My friend Jim Graham, whom I mentioned in the introduction as having great influence on this chapter, tells a story about how his dad discipled him in a single sentence. Jim recalls driving home from church one Wednesday night, just him and his dad. Jim had started dating, and he and his dad had been talking about making godly choices. Jim surmises that there were many other talks before and after that night, but he clearly remembers his dad saying this one, powerful sentence: "I've never been with any other woman except your mother, and there have been times where that has made all the difference." Incredibly personal and intimate? Yes. But powerful enough to pass on a conviction that Jim has kept his entire life, and one he has passed on to his own children.

Discipleship at Home Risks Rejection

- Listen, my son, to your father's instruction and do not forsake your mother's teaching. – Proverbs 1:8

- There is no fear in love. But perfect love drives out fear, because fear has to do with punishment. The one who fears is not made perfect in love. – 1 John 4:18

The intimacy we just discussed is not without risks for parents or for youth workers. And the greatest of those risks is rejection. If you ever watched the old sitcom, *Everybody Loves Raymond*, you know that one of the ongoing bits was the way in which Patricia Heaton, who played Ray's wife, would reject Ray's amorous advances. Ray Romano's character would then exude feelings of insecurity and inadequacy. Although humorously portrayed, the situation reflects the very real emotional risk that we take when we desire intimate interaction with others. The more vulnerable we allow ourselves to be, the greater the risk and fear of rejection.

When adults disciple teenagers at a meaningful level, we are passing on more than information; we are communicating values. Teenagers are still in the process of integrating values into their identity, but adults have already done that. So, when we pass on a value, we are not only saying "this is important," but also "this is who I am." If being at church on Sunday is a priority for parents, and their teenager resists getting up, they may feel rejected by their child. They may further feel embarrassed about themselves when they get to church and well-meaning people, maybe even you, ask, "where's your son?" or say "I haven't seen your daughter in a while." Rejection makes us feel like we have done something wrong, or that there is something wrong with us.

This is especially true for parents trying to initiate spiritual conversations at home. For many parents, these moments are often filled with eye rolling, or body language that make these gatherings frustrating and tense. But, if parents want to pass on their spiritual values and wisdom to their teenagers, they have to continue to make advances despite the risk of rejection. This is true for youth workers, as well. Parents must trust God's plan, believe there will be fruitful results, and risk that their leadership may not be warmly received at first, but that it will ultimately bring blessing on their children.

Discipleship at Home Requires Routine

Luke tells us that traveling to Jerusalem for the Passover was a custom. We know from other events in His life that Jesus was familiar with the synagogue routines as well. This seems to indicate that Mary and Joseph included "going to church" as part of their family's devotional life. Historical tradition tells us that they also had a Sabbath meal, and a day of rest each week. One of the most beneficial practices parents can engage with is to incorporate a steady rhythm or routine in their home as an aspect of discipling. We'll flesh this out some more after we introduce an important counterpart.

Discipleship at Home Is More Everyday Than Special Moments

- When you sit. . . walk. . . lie down . . . get up.
  – Deuteronomy 6:7

- "Come, follow me," Jesus said, "and I will make you fishers of men." At once they left their nets and followed him. – Matthew 4:19-20

In education, we call them "teachable moments." When a teenager raises a question, experiences something that stirs his emotions, or finds herself at a loss about what to do, we have an opportunity for discipleship. We do this all the time. But many parents may miss this because they are not looking. These impromptu, teachable moments are when a parent's own discipleship lessons (what they are learning as a growing disciple) are most easily and naturally passed on. I would say the same truth applies to youth workers.

I believe these two aspects of discipleship – let's call them "routine" and "random" – are two sides of the same coin. As much as circumstances allow, families need to regularly attend church together. Parents committing to participate in the life of the church as an expression of their own faith, and as an opportunity to grow spiritually, communicates volumes to their teenagers. The most involved teenagers are also the ones who get the most benefit. Even when they complain about it (as they do about school, the dentist, and homework), part of parenting is pushing children toward things parents know will ultimately be for their benefit. Discipleship in the home needs to follow a routine.

You can help parents by having a regular, organized plan for discipleship. Hopefully this book has helped you start thinking in that direction. The "formal" experience provides for our students a routine that has significant benefits. First, organized discipleship puts teenagers and adults in the right environment for relationships to develop. Those relationships provide encouragement, accountability, and a sense of belonging that helps teenagers mature. Second, it gives us a way to address aspects of Christian faith, theology, and Christian living through a planned or systematic plan of study. Third, discipleship groups provide the right type of challenge for students who are ready to move to a deeper level of commitment. The training provided in these groups prepares youth for the responsibilities of leadership required to be in the core group.

At the same time, anyone who has done youth ministry for a

while will talk about how many important talks with students happen "after youth group." Teenagers often hang around after the regular events. Some are hoping for a few minutes to talk about something they are working through. The subject may be a million miles away from whatever the group was focused on, but because they want help, it is a wonderful teachable moment. It is my conviction that, without the process of a structured disciplemaking plan, we would not have the relationship connections that allow for this kind of informal discipleship.

For parents, some of the most important discipleship opportunities are also very informal or random. Opportunities like these come in the car after school, or around the kitchen table, or sitting on a bed and talking about life. Many teenagers give pretty vague answers to the question, "how was your day" most of the time, even when we can tell something is wrong. But occasionally they allow a teachable moment when we connect at a deeper level and can share our faith and our hearts.

DISCIPLESHIP AT HOME IS NOT ENOUGH

I hope by this time to have made a convincing, and biblical, case for the parent-child relationship as central to God's plan for discipleship. But the home is not enough. Recently, youth ministry has been under attack in some quarters, replaced by "family-based" structures in which church is viewed as an extension of the family, and fathers bear sole responsibility for spiritually training their children even at church. I strongly believe that the church should not replace the family. But I also believe the family needs the church. Let me briefly touch on several reasons why parents need to partner with, and depend on, the church and youth ministry.

Church (not family) is God's bride. Jesus was very clear that the church is built on the foundation of faith (Matt. 16:18). Although the church is occasionally referred to as "God's family," and we call one another "brother" and "sister" because of biblical examples, the church is most commonly described as a body. The spiritual gifts are given to build up that body (Rom. 12:4-5; 1 Cor. 14:12), as are the various leadership roles (Eph. 4:12-16). When we belong to Christ, we belong to His church, and it is for the church that He will return (Rev. 19:7).

Theologically, the church has a God-given role that is crucial in faith development. The church supports the family, but is also independent of, and biblically superior to, the family in its mission and purpose. Practically, God's design for families is for children to grow until they leave to start a new family. But we never outgrow the church!

Consider the church's role in spiritual leadership gifts. Fathers and mothers have the daily task of passing the faith on to their children, but no father or mother possesses all the spiritual leadership roles God has given. Ephesians 4:11 says some are prophets, pastors, evangelists, preachers, and teachers. These are diverse roles and gifts given for the building of God's people toward maturity and fullness in Christ. Just as a body needs eyes, ears, and hands to be complete, Christians need a variety of leaders and the expression of many spiritual gifts to lead us toward mature faith. You and your youth ministry team fulfill some of these roles. You and parents combine to paint a more complete picture of the church using its gifts to enrich its members' lives and faith.

In 1958, Merton P. Strommen formed the Lutheran Youth Research Center, which is now called The Search Institute. Decades of research among both churched and non-churched teenagers uncovered 40 developmental assets that help children and adolescents become responsible, caring, and healthy. The first two affirm the home: family support and positive family communication. The third crucial asset is "other adult relationships" from outside the home. Teens need meaningful relationships with three or more non-parental adults who echo the values of the home and church for faith to be firmly rooted. (See www.searchinstitute.org for more details and the full list of assets that will benefit your teen). You, your youth ministry team, and the adult volunteers who engage with students are the best example of those meaningful "non-parent" adult relationships.

Further research considered the power of three environments on faith maturity: family, parochial school, and church. Among teenagers who reported caring support in only one of these environments, only 17% demonstrate a maturing faith. 30% of those with two environments offering support gave evidence of mature faith. Fully 53% of those who reported support in all three environments – home, Christian school, and church – expressed a measurably mature faith.[1]

We have probably arrived at the point where we have to ask the question, what about parents who do not have a saving relationship with Jesus? The reality is that millions of teenagers will attend church youth groups who do not have Christian parents to disciple them. The National Survey of Youth and Religion revealed that 69% of all U.S. teens and 86% of conservative Protestant teens (Baptist, Evangelical, Bible, Presbyterian, etc.) have been involved in a youth group. Some 51% of U.S. teens attend a religious service two or more times a month and as many as 55% of conservative Protestant teens (Baptist, Evangelical, Bible, Presbyterian, etc.) attend at least once a week.[2] Among those who attend regularly, as many as one-in-six do so without parental involvement. Without a church youth group that includes a pattern for discipling teenagers, we abandon a huge group that we have "reached" but not matured.

The privilege and responsibility of parents to disciple their children are based on clear, biblical mandates. The necessity of partnering with other adults within the context of a church (and youth group) is equally true from a biblical and practical viewpoint. Parents cannot turn over the responsibility for developing a teenager's spiritual growth to the church; the significance of parental influence and example would never be outdone by even the best of youth group experiences. At the same time, churches must have a systematic plan and process for nurturing spiritual growth in partnership with the family, while taking care of those whose parents cannot or do not provide Christian discipleship in the home. Fathers and mothers must set aside time for intentional disciple-making in the family, which serves as a springboard for the informal, daily opportunities to pass on the faith.

In light of questions, I thought giving a list of suggestions for parents might be helpful. Consider passing these along to the parents of the students in your youth ministry.

SUGGESTIONS FOR PARENTS

1. Set aside at least one time each week to have a family devotional that includes Bible reading and prayer.

2. Use daily opportunities to talk about faith.

3. Plan a regular one-on-one time with each family member to foster relationships, discuss life, and enjoy each other's company.

4. Support the church and youth group efforts to provide spiritual growth experiences, such as camps, retreats, or on-going Bible study groups as a family priority.

5. Work on parental harmony; marital discord has an overwhelming effect on family disunity.

6. Practice effective communication with your teenager in all areas to pave the way for discipling. Teach your son or daughter active listening skills, and practice verbalizing emotions.

7. Provide expanding opportunities for teen independence based on proven responsibility.

8. Parental control is important, but move toward the goal of internalized self-control as a milestone to reach before the college-years.

9. Foster close family relationships. Parents who express a high level of care balanced by a low level of protectiveness (allowing autonomy and individual responsibility) produce children with the highest levels of psychological adjustment and faith maturity.

CHAPTER 6:

A CLOSING: "MY NAME IS ALLEN AND I WILL BE YOUR SERVER . . ."

I live in New Orleans, a place famous for food. So, when someone asks me, "Where is the best place to eat in New Orleans?" I usually respond, "Well, what do you want to eat?" Do you want seafood (fried or grilled)? Do you want steak (Ruth's Chris started here, but, then again, we also have Golden Corral)? Do you want something Cajun or Creole (red beans and rice, jambalaya, shrimp étouffée, gumbo)? Do you want a New Orleans specialty like char-grilled oysters at Drago's, or a prime rib po' boy at Crazy Johnny's? Do you want dessert? How about a donut the size of a Frisbee at Daddy's Donuts? Or white chocolate bread pudding at Coffee Cottage? Or beignets at Café Du Monde?

Pardon me. I just got a little carried away. You have my permission to go raid the pantry. (Or call your travel agent.) Now that you are back and ready to read, I will let you in on a secret. I didn't exactly know how to finish this book up. I had several ideas. Most of them were shorter than a chapter, and longer than a sentence. And I was afraid that not all of my ideas would apply to all of you.

So I decided, in the best New Orleans Tradition, to finish the book with a chapter that is a little like a menu. My name is Allen and I will be your server. Look over the menu and see what you feel like reading first. It may be that you want to read everything in this chapter. It may be that you want to look through the headings and see if something catches your eye. Plan your first course, your second course, and so on. Be sure to leave room for dessert. The sections are designed to be self-contained, and still give direction to the process of disciplemaking.

I hope you've enjoyed this book. I enjoyed writing it for you.

APPETIZERS

Relationships in Disciplemaking

Relationships cannot have strings attached. We cannot be in the lives of students only so that we can disciple them. If we are in a relationship with students in order to impact them spiritually, what happens if they aren't interested? Do we abandon the relationship if they are not interested? I have heard Dr. Andrew Root[1] speak on relationships in youth ministry. His book, *Relationships Unfiltered*, points out that if relationships are used as tools where adults try to influence students to accept, know, trust, believe, or participate in something, they are insincere. While our desire (appropriately) is to see students mature in Christ (the whole point of this book), we cannot focus so much on their progress that we miss them as people.

The Disciplemaker as a Teacher
In my world as a professor, we talk about learning on three levels, or domains. We learn by taking in information (the cognitive domain). We learn by developing a passion or urgency about something (the affective). We learn by developing a new skill or behavior (the psychomotor). A disciplemaker as a teacher is aware that the "stuff" of discipleship is cognitive (information about the person of Jesus), affective (falling in love with Jesus and being crazy about following Him), and psychomotor (devotional practices, spiritual discipline).

A teacher uses all the tools available–methods, illustration, parable, project, discussion, storytelling in order to make the content come alive, and passion–to lead students in discipleship.

Discipleship as Curriculum
In terms of most things in youth ministry, curriculum has a bad reputation. "It's a horrible curriculum, so I don't pay any attention to the book!" "Trying to do all of the activities in the curriculum is just too much work." These statements, and others like them, are evidence that folks are confusing curriculum with literature. Literature is the printed material. Curriculum is everything that is done to get the lesson into the life of the learner. I usually define curriculum as "a path to run on," or "a race course."

Introducing The 21st Century Teen
This is a link to my free e-book on adolescent development I mentioned way back in chapter 1. It's a quick read. I pray it helps you better understand the students you're ministering to.

http://media.wix.com/ugd/a64705_8e080a932baeba52503e7f-b1ebe1f80e.pdf

ENTREES

Discipleship of Adults

Who is discipling adults, many of them parents, who will in turn disciple teenagers? It serves to reason that if the expectation is that adults (you, dear reader) are disciplemakers to students, a plan should be in place to disciple adults. Food for thought from veteran youth minister, Jared Osborne.[2]

An Open Letter to Youth Ministers by Jared Osborne
I've been in student ministry since 2002 fighting to save the world with every breath. Sundays, Wednesdays, events, and office hours flew by as the years piled up. After 12 years, I received a gut check from the Holy Spirit that is currently running its course through our entire ministry. As a staff, we decided to start doing that one thing that ministers all talk about doing, but, honestly, we never really do. We said, "Let's entrust the Gospel to our people. What if we equipped every disciple to make disciples?" This question has birthed an intentional practice for our students and adult leaders: Multiplication. It's giving the great commission back to the people by equipping them to reproduce the process.

We started two years ago with two adults and two students. I personally taught these groups, and sent them out to replicate the process. This past year 12 people became disciple-makers, investing in 30 other people, who will, in turn, be able to teach others.

Multiplication
This has been a compelling experience, but we knew there had to be more. As a part of our year-end evaluation, we found that our adult leadership was not intimately involved. Therefore, this summer we are raising the bar by training our adult leadership. Each adult leader connected to our ministry will be challenged to commit to teaching two other adults to become fishers of men. Once equipped these adults will actively train two other adults to repeat the process. Multiplication.

Go, Baptize, Teach
We want to change the scoreboard in student ministry from, "how many are here?" to "how many are reproducing?" My fear is that we would do the ministry without the people. All around us ministries are growing and churches are multiplying, but have the people become marginalized? Disciplemaking cannot be ignored. Join me as I fight to give back the great commission to the people who the Spirit of God has empowered to save the world.

Information vs. Imputation

The industrialization of student ministry has increased personnel and pushed out the parent. If done poorly, our paid staff can meet the ministry quota without including the body of Christ. Production does not drop, but people are no longer an intricate part of the process. It begins to taste a lot like the automatization of America, and nobody's got a job anymore. Let's put people back to work. Why do we teach kids to listen to what we preach instead of teaching them to teach others?

Personal Pursuit

Thursdays changed my life. 10 years ago Dr. Jason Lee invited me and another young guy on our staff to discuss Scripture with him every week. For the next year or so he invested deeply into our lives. Little did I know he was "teaching others (us) to obey also." He offered to me something that I had not found before in a Bible study or a sermon. He taught me to me how to read the Scriptures for myself. He taught me good theology and he let me ask questions. I was introduced to Bonhoeffer, Luther, and books like *Christ and Culture* by Richard Niebuhr. Thursdays were intentional, directional, and measurable. Looking back, I was Timothy, and Dr. Lee was Paul.

I attended conferences and read more books. Then I personally started discipling a few students and a few adults. This was different from any small group I had ever done in the past. The goal was to pass on the Gospel to others so they could do this for somebody else.

Why had we not been doing it like this before?

A Progression of Maturity in Discipleship.

What would a discipleship "course" look like? It is creating environments through intentional relationships, handling intentional materials, embarking on intentional mission projects, and sustaining an intentional trajectory towards maturity. I think that one of the most remarkable examples of a discipleship curriculum is found in Matthew 5-7. It is a part of the Scripture we call the Sermon on the Mount, and the part I want to look at is called "The Beatitudes." A teacher might ask, "how do you guide a teenager from being a new Christian (poor in spirit) to maturity (persecuted for the sake of the name of Jesus) in a systematic and intentional way?"

My mentor, Dennis Rogers, showed me this in a Bible study while

I was still in college and I have found other writers who see it the same way (though not all do). Each statement is like a step toward maturity (one writer called them "rungs on a ladder"). Each one, in my view, leads to the next.

The steps aren't in a random order. To reach the second step, we need to make the first step. Maybe it will be helpful to you as it was to me to look at them this way.

Blessed are the poor in spirit, for theirs is the kingdom of heaven.
I'm talking about being poor spiritually and knowing that you are poor. When students realize that they need forgiveness and grace, they can call on God and be saved. There's an understanding that they cannot save themselves with knowledge or good deeds. Neither money, nor power will cleanse us before God, only our awareness that we desperately need Jesus. Peter wrote in 1 Peter 1:3,

> Blessed be the God and Father of our Lord Jesus Christ, who according to His great mercy has caused us to be born again to a living hope through the resurrection of Jesus Christ from the dead (NASB).

According to His great mercy, God caused us to be born again. We could not help ourselves.

Blessed are those who mourn, for they will be comforted.
Students begin to see their responsibility in their own sin. The old cliché says, "The devil made me do it." While the evil one has a part in our sin, the choices are ours. Our sinful condition was not created from without by bad leaders, laws, or circumstances, but from within. The goal is for our students to confess (the word means "to agree") and to be broken over their spiritual condition. Confession is one thing. But contrition is another.

Blessed are the meek, for they will inherit the earth.
Meekness has been pictured as the bit in the mouth of a thoroughbred racehorse. It is a controlling influence on a very powerful animal. It means, "strength under control" and does not refer to weakness. Our teenagers are powerful in their wills and potential, but they must realize their strength needs to be under God's control. Students begin to subject their priorities to Him and allow Him to direct their paths.

Blessed are those who hunger and thirst for righteousness, for they will be filled.

Students begin to be hungry and thirsty for the things found in God's kitchen. They begin to desire things that are of God. A popular praise song says, "Break my heart for what breaks yours." As our students respond to others with the patience and love that God is developing in their lives, they find a freedom of spirit. Righteous is being right for the right reasons.

Blessed are the merciful, for they will be shown mercy.
Many of us know situations where people have become rich or powerful by causing others to suffer. We are offended by the violence or abuse we see. Many of us (me) are at least initially inclined to want those people to suffer in the same way they have caused suffering. Yet in Jesus is a constant example of someone ready to be merciful to anyone, no matter what that person has done. Whether a woman condemned to death for adultery, or a thief on an adjacent cross, Jesus extends mercy. When our students, too, extend undeserved kindness, they breathe a different kind of air, one with the fragrance of mercy.

Blessed are the pure in heart, for they will see God.
What is a pure heart? John Stott called it "utterly sincere." A pure heart is a heart given to God's definition of purity, a heart able to mourn, a heart that thirsts for what is right, a heart that is merciful, a heart that doesn't look at people merely as objects to be used. The hope here is that our students would begin to see pornography for what it is, immorality as God sees it, and injustice as an offense. A pure heart means we began to see God Himself working in us and through us.

Blessed are the peacemakers, for they will be called sons of God.
The journey toward maturity is evident. A disciple has to get involved in making peace. A pure hearted person who has seen God, and been drawn in by His love, is motivated to break down walls and restore or build relationship. Disciples do not seek peace because it is a good deed, or benefits them personally, but because they see each person—even the nasty ones—as someone made in the image of and loved by God.

Blessed are you when people insult you, persecute you and falsely say all kinds of evil against you because of me. Rejoice and be glad, because great is your reward in heaven, for in the same way they persecuted the prophets who were before you.

To rejoice in persecution or trials (James 1) is a price to be paid for being faithful to our King. The disciple is not thanked for his efforts but is often opposed, insulted, excluded, ridiculed, and persecuted on account of the declaration as a follower of Christ.

What if our students were progressively shaped by the radical teachings of Jesus, especially here in the Sermon on the Mount? What if teenagers were distinctly and increasingly different in the way they relate to God (poor in spirit, mourning for our failures, allowing Him to control our strength, desperate for His righteousness in our culture)?

10 Discipleship Truths (Learned the Hard Way)[3]

I have been doing youth ministry for something like 14 years. I like to think I have learned a little bit of the right way, and the wrong way, to do things. Mostly what I have learned is that there is still a lot to be learned. But maybe that's another article for another day. For today, here are 10 truths about leading others, specifically teenagers, in a discipleship journey.

1. I have at times overestimated the effect of my influence on the lives of teenagers whom I have discipled. Discipleship happens primarily because the Spirit is working in the lives of students. The older I get the more thankful I am that this is true.

2. A friend of mine used to say that discipleship was "crockpot stuff," not "microwave stuff." This great little analogy has stuck with me over the years. It reminds me to be patient, and to take a long-term view of things.

3. Discipleship doesn't happen in a vacuum. Teenagers' lives are a complex system where parents, friends, other adults, and their immediate cultural contexts all contribute to impact their faith. We are only one of many voices.

4. Life-on-life discipleship is fun. If you're not having fun with your students, you're doing it wrong.

5. Life-on-life discipleship is not always fun. If you're not occasionally walking through the valley, you're not doing it right.

6. Agendas are rarely a positive thing. When we come into a relationship with a preconceived image of what someone's spiritual life should look like, frustration (and sometimes pain) is sure to follow.

7. Discipleship can't happen without knowledge. We have to know God to follow Him. But I have at times in the past made discipleship more about knowledge than action. I think discipleship is about knowledge informing action. It's helping teenagers see how knowing God can literally transform their actions and attitudes.

8. I have benefited immensely from reading about discipleship practices and philosophy. But much if not most of it gets tossed out the window when you're trying to study the Bible with five 7th grade boys.

9. Discipleship is every bit about tomorrow as it is about today. I want my teenage guys to be influencers and leaders today for the sake of Christ. But I also want them to be awesome husbands and fathers. I hope to play a small role on both ends of the spectrum.

10. I like to think about the discipleship journey in terms of proximity. In essence, we attempt to lead teenagers closer to Christ. Most of the time this is done beside them, journeying with them as they go. Often were close behind them, gently pushing them in the right direction. Occasionally we're in front, pulling them where they need to go. And every once in a while, we're far behind, watching them lead out. These are the best times.

Discipleship That Stuck

I hear a lot about young adults who abandon the church and faith after they leave home. I decided to ask Seminary students–young adults who did not abandon the church, or faith– why they stuck around. I asked every student in my classes to write an open-ended essay about their life between elementary school and Seminary. One hundred students turned in an essay. My research method was qualitative, in that I took different-colored highlighters to mark similarities in their stories. Their testimonies fell into 3 categories:

- Some students never "strayed," though some of them went through a "disconnected," or "apathetic," season in their faith journey.

- Some students had returned from a walk on the wild side. Some wilder than others.

• Some students came to faith after high school.

About 75% of them indicated that their parents or grandparents were influential in faith formation. All who indicated that family faith was strong, described it as "authentic," though some described parents as "controlling." About half indicated that "surrogate," or other adults besides parents (extended family, church, community), were influential. They described adult volunteers in youth ministry as "mentors."

I rarely heard that church was positive unless friends were mentioned. Most worked 10+hours per week or played varsity sports. If family was not the catalyst for faith, then it was friend influence. "Youth group" was mentioned more positively than "church." 100% who were far from God, either because they strayed, or because they were lost, were "brought back" by a friend. Even the young adults who never strayed indicated the presence of a spiritual mentor

Most interesting in my conversations was that the ninth/tenth grade year was pivotal in their discipleship. More than three-quarters of the students indicated that something significant happened in ninth grade.

• "I became a Christian at camp"

• "I knew I was called to ministry"

• "I knew it was real on a mission trip"

It looked to me like that was the time in their adolescent growth (back to chapter 2) that they were able to process abstract thought, in terms of application, and they had someone there to guide them. A disciplemaker was there to marry the lessons of life with the lessons of Jesus.

Traits of a Disciple[4]
Another way to look at discipleship is to look at what a disciple might look like. Did you follow all that? One of the most powerful ways to actually be a disciplemaker is to actually be a disciple. There I went again. But you get it, right? When you are modeling a lifestyle that has Jesus at the middle of it, and the priorities of discipleship as observable habits, students are able to see a realistic expression of a Jesus-follower in their culture.

Discipleship Trait 1: Surrender To A Gospel-Centered Life
Being a Christian isn't about being a good person. There are plenty of good people in this world. And being a Christian isn't all about what God can do for you (or your students). Being a Christian is ultimately about surrender. It's about giving up the control of our lives and letting God lead, as He alone is uniquely suited to lead.

Discipleship Trait 2: Hunger To Know God
A secular Christianity emerges when our actions are motivated by working to be "moral," instead of seeking to imitate Christ. This kind of legalism is common among students and adults who are still maturing in their faith. As we grow in Christ-like-ness, we need to help our students move away from legalism and toward a desire to live like Christ. But the tough reality is that our teenagers can't imitate God if they don't know what He looks like.

Discipleship Trait 3: Embrace Christian Community
Christian community is more than just hanging out. Relationships are vital to our lives, but Christian community is deeper than friendship. Christian community is the God-given space in which we're supposed to live our lives. You might call it "church." Discipleship is modeled across generations. Community is different than mere friendship. It is life-connection around the person of Jesus.

Discipleship Trait 4: Engage With Our Surroundings
As Christ-followers, we are called to engage our families, neighborhood, city, country, and the world in the name of Christ. This is the Gospel in action (wait for trait #6). This is "compassionate awareness" of bringing Christ into all of our environments. Some call this being "missional."

Discipleship Trait 5: Desire To Worship God
A desire to worship God goes beyond what we do in "big church" on Sunday mornings. For you and your students, worship should be understood as simply this: a right response to who God is. We all encounter Jesus in various ways–the Bible, nature, interaction with family or friends, and so on. Worship is a response when we refuse to keep God in the "church" category and see Him in every part of our lives.

Discipleship Trait 6: Invest In Multiplying Disciples
There are two types of multiplication in talking about discipleship: kingdom multiplication and individual multiplication.

Kingdom multiplication is what happens in a big sense because someone is a Christ follower. It is what my mentor called "distinctive differentness" in the way we conduct our business. Personal evangelism, is generally "life-on-life," and happens when you or your students seek out the lost in a sphere of influence and invite them into their journey.

DESSERT

Great Quotes Regarding Discipleship

"Jesus calls us to his rest, and meekness is His method. The meek man cares not at all who is greater than he, for he has long ago decided that the esteem of the world is not worth the effort."
– A.W. Tozer, *Pursuit of God*

"For those who feel their lives are a grave disappointment to God, it requires enormous trust and reckless, raging confidence to accept that the love of Jesus Christ knows no shadow of alteration or change. When Jesus said, "Come to me, all you who labor and are heavy burdened," He assumed we would grow weary, discouraged, and disheartened along the way."
– Brennan Manning, *The Ragamuffin Gospel: Good News for the Bedraggled, Beat-Up, and Burnt Out*

"The goal of religion is to comfort the afflicted and afflict the comfortable."
– Archbishop of Canterbury (maybe, but even Wikipedia won't verify this one. Originally the quote came from Finley Peter Dunne (1867-1936) to refer to journalism, but has been modified and edited through the years, especially by preachers. It rings remarkably true in thinking about a goal of discipleship as well.)

"Discipleship is not an offer that man makes to Christ."
– Dietrich Bonhoeffer, *The Cost of Discipleship*.

"Discipleship is developing a personal, lifelong, obedient relationship with Jesus Christ in which He transforms your character into Christlikeness; changes your values to Kingdom values; and involves you in His mission in the home, in the church, and in the world."
– Avery T. Willis Jr., several sources.

The Disciplemaker as a Leader

New Orleans is home to the National World War II museum. It is humbling and inspiring to go through (I am a charter member), and for me it never gets old. One of my favorite pictures is that of General Eisenhower visiting the paratroopers who would jump over Normandy on D-Day. The man he is talking to has just turned 22, and is identified as a "jump captain," which I later learned is responsible for telling troops when to jump out of the airplane.

My first thought was, "Don't tell me that a generation of students does not have the willpower, motivation, and ability to lead. Here is a man who sends other men out of an airplane and he is barely an adult by today's standards." On a recent trip to the museum with my daughter, Sarah, a young adult, I saw a quote on the wall that talks about leading such soldiers:

> "When you talk about combat leadership under fire on the beach at Normandy, I don't see how the credit can go to anyone other than the company-grade officers, and senior NCOs who led the way. It is good to be reminded that there are such men, that there always have been, and always will be. We sometimes forget, I think, that you can manufacture weapons, and you can purchase ammunition, but you can't buy valor, and you can't pull heroes off an assembly line." – Sgt. John Ellery, 16th Infantry Regiment, U.S. 1st Division

A Prayer to Close

Jesus, thank you for allowing us to be your disciples. As we attempt to guide students to discipleship, give us wisdom, courage, patience, and creativity. Lead us to students who need to be discipled, who want to be discipled, and who will be challenged in the hard things of discipleship. Allow us to be lifelong disciples and learners. Put people in our path that will teach us, challenge us, and lead us. We know the future is in your hands. Thank you for allowing us to be part of the story. Amen.

END NOTES

Chapter 1
1. Rick Lawrence, "The Sacred Dreams Of Teenagers," Group November-December 2011.

2. Warren W. Wiersbe, *The Bible Exposition Commentary, Volume 1*: Matthew-Galatians (Colorado Springs, CO: David C. Cook, 1989).

3. Eugene Peterson, *A Long Obedience in the Same Direction* (Downers Grove, Il.: InterVarsity Press, 1980 (1st ed) and 2000 (2nd ed)).

4. Psalm 121:1-2. My paraphrase.

5. Several sources report this to be Mishnah Aboth 1:4.

Chapter 2
1. Dr. Seuss, *Horton Hears A Who* (New York, NY: Random House, 1954, 1982).

2. http://www.nbcnews.com/news/u-news/meet-joe-millennial-optimistic-independent-facebook-n47251

3. Avery Willis and Mark Snowden, *Truth that Sticks: How To Communicate Velcro Truth In A Teflon World* (Colorado Springs, CO: NavPress, 2010).

Chapter 3
1. John Blanchard, ed., *The Complete Gathered Gold, A treasury of quotations for Christians* (Webster, New York: Evangelical Press, 2006).

2. Chuck Swindoll, *Growing Strong in the Seasons of Life* (Grand Rapids: Zondervan, 1994).

3. https://www.biblegateway.com/blog/2013/03/ten-tips-for-memorizing-bible-verses/

4. Leroy Eims, *The Lost Art of Disciplemaking* (Grand Rapids, MI.: Zondervan Publishing House, 1978).

5. Joshua Stanton, Social Justice in the Millennial Generation, blog post on http://www.huffingtonpost.com/joshua-stanton/ social-justice-in-the-mil_b_2708224.html, posted 2/17/2013, accessed October 25, 2014.

6. Ibid.

7. John Stott, *Christian Counter Culture* (Westmont, Ill.: Intervarsity Press), 1978.

8. John Stott, *The Radical Disciple* (Westmont, Ill.: Intervarsity Press), 2010.

9. David Crosby, Not the Social Gospel, blog Post September 2, 2014. Found at http://www.fbno.org/pastors-blog/, Accessed 10 September 2014.

10. Rick Lawrence, *Jesus-Centered Youth Ministry* (Loveland, CO: Group Publishing Company, 2014).

11. Ibid.

Chapter 4

1. Willard, Dallas, *The Great Omission: Reclaiming Jesus' Essential Teachings on Discipleship* (San Francisco: Harper Collins, 2006).

2. https://www.entheos.com/philosophersnotes/notes/all/ The-Selected-Writings-of-Ralph-Waldo-Emerson. Accessed September 10, 2014.

3. Donald S. Whitney, *Spiritual Disciplines For The Christian Life* (Colorado Springs, CO: NavPress, 1991).

4. Chap Clark, Kara Powell, S*ticky Faith: Everyday Ideas To Build Lasting Faith In Your Kids* (Grand Rapids, MI: Zondervan, 2011).

5. Rosalind Rinker, Prayer: *Conversing With God* (Grand Rapids, MI: Zondervan, 1959).

6. Georgia Harkness, *Prayer And The Common Life* (Nashville, TN: Abingdon Press, 1948).

7. http://www.dwillard.org/articles/artview.asp?artID=40, Accessed September 17, 2014. Originally published in *The Great*

Omission (San Francisco: HarperCollins, 2006).

8. http://www.intouch.org/magazine/content.aspx?topic=The_Spiritual_Discipline_of_Fasting_devotional#.VBm4bMJdXHQ

9. Dallas Willard, *The Spirit of the Disciplines* (San Francisco: Harper Collins, 1999).

10. Richard Foster *Celebration of Discipline* (San Francisco: Harper Collins, 1978, 1988, 1998).

Chapter 5

1. Merton P. Strommen and Richard A. Hardel, *Passing On the Faith: A Radical New Model for Youth and Family Ministry* (Winona, MN: St. Mary's Press, 2000).

2. Christian Smith, *Soul Searching: The Religious and Spiritual Lives of American Teenagers* (New York, NY: Oxford University Press, 2005).

Chapter 6

1. Andrew Root is the Olson Baalson Associate Professor of Youth and Family Ministry and teaches at Luther Seminary in St. Paul, MN. *Relationships Unfiltered* was published by Youth Specialties in 2009. He speaks and writes on issues of pastoral and practical theology.

2. Jared is High School Pastor, Broadmoor Baptist Church, Shreveport, LA.

3. Andy is the co-founder of ym360. He loves Jesus, his wife, their four kids, and baseball. In that order. youthministry360 The Magazine Fall 2014 Issue 03.

4. Adapted from Andy Blanks, *The Six Biblical Discipleship Traits: A Framework For Thinking About How We Disciple Teenagers* ©2014 by youthministry360. All rights reserved.

ACKNOWLEDGMENTS

This book came out of discussions with my former student, colleague, and (above all) friend, Jim Graham. The chapter on discipleship in the church and home is mostly Jim's ideas. I am always sharpened when I am in the same space with Jim. He is analytical, philosophical, creative, and selfless. Youth ministry is better because Jim has spoken into so many lives, usually behind the scenes.

I am indebted to my bride, Dr. Judi Jackson, who listens to my rants, challenges my biases, and makes my home a safe place to just be. I love the continuing adventure that ministry is. The reality of a soulmate to share it with is what gives me the confidence for this and every initiative. My adult children, Aaron and Sarah, continue to give me "real" perspective on my writing, teaching, and speaking.

Andy and Les—editors, publishers, and friends—are more than a place to print a book. They genuinely desire to connect youth ministers with the best resources to help them, whether it is a youth-ministry360 resource, or not. I appreciate the way they massaged the content so that it would sound a little less like an old man wrote the book. Which he did.

I am grateful to Dr. Chuck Kelley for the environment at the New Orleans Baptist Theological Seminary, which allows, and encourages me to write and speak. My team in the Youth Ministry Institute through the years has made me appear much better than I could ever be. Thank you.

Allen Jackson
New Orleans Louisiana
February 2015

ABOUT THE AUTHOR

Dr. Allen Jackson is Professor of Youth Ministry at the New Orleans Baptist Theological Seminary. Allen came to the Crescent City in 1994 after being in several local churches as minister to students. His job at the seminary is to be a youth minister to youth ministers. He has done interim work as a pastor and as a youth pastor since coming to the seminary. He is the founder and director of the Youth Ministry Institute (www.youthministryinstitute.org).

Allen works hard to stay on top of the issues that face youth and youth ministers. He is a volunteer youth worker at his church (FBC New Orleans) when he is not doing an interim ministry somewhere, which he has been doing off and on for 12 years. He still leads Disciple Nows, teaches small groups, preaches youth camps, conducts research on teenagers . . . whatever he can do to know what's impacting teenagers and their faith.

Allen is a Texan by birth, but spent significant growing-up years in Georgia, Mississippi, and Louisiana. He has a business degree from the University of Southern Mississippi in Accounting, a Master of Religious Education and a PhD from the New Orleans Seminary.

Allen has written extensively for youth publications including *Straight Trak Teen Bible Studies, Countdown: 20 Bible Studies for High School Seniors, Help! Peer Pressure,* Youthworker Journal, and Group magazine. Has authored numerous books including *Teach: The Ordinary Person's Guide To Teaching The Bible; Connected, Committed and a Little Bit Crazy* (with Randy Johnson); *Leaders, Lessons and Lifestyles; Introducing the 21st Century Teenager; Followology at Collegiate Ministry;* and *Into Their Shoes.* He's contributed a chapter in *Basic Youth Ministry,* as well as a bunch of other stuff. He writes a column entitled, "Ask Allen" for Leading Students magazine. He also served on the original Board of Directors for what was Student Life Bible Study.

Become A Better Bible Teacher.
Here's How.

Teenagers need to know God. The Bible is the best way to get to know Him. And so, teaching the Bible is a vital skill for youth workers.

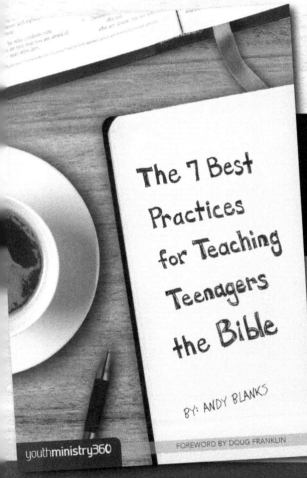

The 7 Best Practices For Teaching Teenagers The Bible **is one of the best resources available for helping youth workers know how to teach God's Word.**

The 7 Best Practices for Teaching Teenagers the Bible

BY: ANDY BLANKS

FOREWORD BY DOUG FRANKLIN

youthministry360

To sample the book, or to order, go to youthministry360.com/7-best-practices

13 STUDIES TO CHOOSE FROM

Up to 52 Weeks of Material

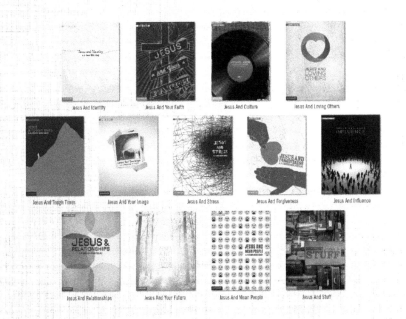

Help teens see what Jesus says about
pressing, day-to-day, real life issues.

To get started with the Jesus Studies,
go to youthministry360.com/jesus-studies